AFORE THE HIGHLANDS

The Jacobites in Perth, 1715-16

KATHLEEN LYLE

TIPPERMUIR
· BOOKS LIMITED ·

Afore the Highlands: The Jacobites in Perth, 1715-16
by Kathleen Lyle. Copyright © 2019. All rights reserved.

The right of Kathleen Lyle to be identified as the author of the Work
has been asserted by her in accordance with the
Copyright, Designs & Patents Act 1988.
This first edition published and copyright 2019 by
Tippermuir Books Ltd, Perth, Scotland.
mail@tippermuirbooks.co.uk
www.tippermuirbooks.co.uk

ISBN-13: 978-1-9164778-3-4 (paperback)
ISBN-10: 1-9164778-3-6
A CIP catalogue record for this book is available from the British Library.

Project coordination by Paul S. Philippou.
Cover design by Matthew Mackie.
Additional map by Rob Hands
Additional photography by Roben Antoniewicz.
Text design, layout and artwork by Bernard Chandler [graffik].
Text set in Adobe Caslon Pro 11/14pt with Wyld [Caslon] titling.
Printed and Bound by CPI Group (UK) Ltd, Croydon, CR0 4YY.

ACKNOWLEDGEMENTS

I WOULD LIKE TO THANK the library staff (Local & Family History) of Perth's AK Bell Library, and offer a special thanks to the staff of Perth & Kinross Archive who have always been helpful and welcoming. I am also grateful to everyone at the Department of Continuing Education in Oxford, especially my supervisor Dr Stewart Tolley. Thanks also to Paul Philippou of Tippermuir Books for his help and encouragement in developing my research material into a book. And also to Rob Hands for his map of Perthshire and Matthew Mackie for the cover.

CONTENTS

Preface
List of Illustrations
Notes to the Reader
Map 1

PREFACE

FOR A FEW MONTHS in 1715–16, when it was occupied by Jacobite forces, Perth was at a focal point of British and European history. Despite its importance, it is a part of the city's past that has been largely forgotten.

Perth, which then had a population of around 5,000, became the headquarters for an army of perhaps 10,000 men. Where were they all accommodated? How were they fed? What did the townspeople think of the occupation? Did they all support the Jacobite cause? Questions like this are not often addressed by existing histories of the 1715 rising, which tend to concentrate on military events or national politics.

In this book I have attempted to piece together information from a wide range of sources to illuminate details of the Jacobite occupation of Perth and some other aspects of the 1715 rising. The reports are widely scattered in archives and published sources such as contemporary newspapers and books, family histories, and collections of letters and documents. Fortunately, it is much easier to research the Jacobite period now than it would have been a generation ago. Literally thousands of eighteenth- and nineteenth-century publications that are rare and hard to find in libraries are now available to download from the internet, usually free. Although archive material itself is rarely available online, the catalogues of public archives often are, making them available for everyone to search. The parish records on the National Records of Scotland's website, 'ScotlandsPeople', are another invaluable resource.

Scotland in the early eighteenth century was a highly stratified society. The mass of the population were poor, illiterate, and had no voice in local or national politics. Even with access to so many sources, it is not easy to find out what was happening to ordinary men, far less ordinary women. Contemporary chroniclers usually did not think it necessary to mention them; except when they are accused of a crime or misdemeanour, they rarely appear in the written records of the burgh or the parish. What life must have been like for them in occupied Perth in the cold and hungry winter of 1715/16 can only be imagined.

Kathleen Lyle, Oxford, June 2019

LIST OF ILLUSTRATIONS

COVER IMAGE

DETAIL FROM A MAP BY JOHN ADAIR: *'The Mapp of Straithern,
Stormount, and Cars of Gourie, with the Rivers Tay and Jern' /
surveighed and designed by J. Adair; James Moxon sculp.'.*
[EMS.s.320 - Reproduced by permission of the National Library of Scotland.]

MAPS

FIGURES

FIGURE 5 *Pages 64–65:* Account of the Glover Incorporation's expenditure for Henry Laing *'on going out for the trade to the town companies'*.
[Reproduced by permission of Perth & Kinross Archives MS67/17/Bundle 177.]

FIGURE 6 *Page 108:* A document printed in Perth by Robert Freebairn: a handbill issued by the Earl of Mar, requiring heritors to provide grain for the Jacobite army, 24 November 1715 (SP 54/10/78). Note that double the amount is demanded from those who are not *'in the King's* [i.e. James's] *service'*.
[Reproduced by permission of The National Archives.]

FIGURE 7 *Page 118:* James arriving at Peterhead in December 1715, as imagined by a Dutch artist. [Image in Public Domain.]

NOTES TO THE READER

SPELLING AND PUNCTUATION

Eighteenth-century spelling is best described as idiosyncratic. The spelling even of proper names is often phonetic and can vary between and within documents. I have kept the original spelling in extracts from contemporary sources to give a flavour of the speech of the time. For example, the Master of Sinclair always writes 'Pearth' for Perth, and anyone familiar with the local accent will understand why.

OLD STYLE AND NEW STYLE DATES

By 1715, most countries in western Europe had adopted the Gregorian calendar but Britain and its colonies retained the old Julian calendar until 1752. This resulted in an eleven-day difference with mainland Europe in 1715 and 1716. Some correspondence and some key dates cited in this text stem from mainland Europe and consequently use 'New Style' (N.S.) dating. In these cases, the 'Old Style' (O.S.) date of the British Isles is added. In some cases, the date style is stated explicitly, to avoid ambiguity.

STYLES AND TITLES

During his long life, James Francis Edward Stuart (1685–1766) played many roles under many different names. As the baby son of James II, he was proclaimed Prince of Wales; in France, where he grew up, he was recognised by Louis XIV as James III of Great Britain on his father's death in 1701 but assumed the title of Chevalier de St George when serving with the French army. While he was still in exile in France, the Earl of Mar proclaimed him King James VIII of Scotland. To his English adherents he was James III, but to Whigs he was the Pretender. In 1745 and after he was known as the Old Pretender to distinguish him from his son Charles Edward Louis John Casimir Sylvester Severino Maria Stuart, the Young Pretender, now popularly known as Bonnie Prince Charlie. Whigs who wished to be polite to Jacobite sympathisers, or Jacobites who wished to avoid trouble, might refer to either Pretender as 'the Chevalier'.

Heritors (landowners) were usually called by the name of their estate rather than by their surname. This avoided confusion when there were many men of the same surname in an area. For example, Mr Oliphant of Gask was addressed as Gask and although he had no title his wife was generally referred to as Lady Gask rather than Mrs Oliphant.

The heir to a title in the Scottish peerage is traditionally known as Master. The Master of Sinclair was heir to his father, Lord Sinclair.

SCOTS CURRENCY

Although the old Scots currency technically went out of use at the time of the Union with England in 1707, in practice it was still widely used for many years after that. In documents of the Jacobite period, sums of money are usually in Scots currency unless specifically designated as sterling. Sterling amounts were most often used for official payments of some kind. At the time of the Union, the Scots pound was valued at one-twelfth of the pound sterling. For small sums the conversion to pre-decimal sterling is simple: one shilling (1s. or 1/-) Scots is equal to one penny (1d.) sterling. In legal documents of the period, sums of money are often designated in merks. One merk was worth two-thirds of a pound, or 13s. 4d. Scots (approximately 1s. 1½d. sterling). By the eighteenth century, the merk was used only as a unit of account, although there had been coins of this denomination in the past.

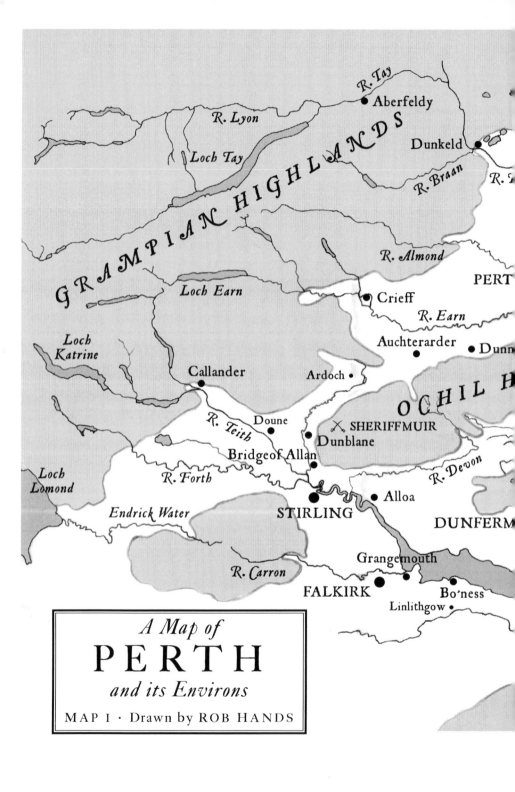

A Map of
PERTH
and its Environs
MAP I · Drawn by ROB HANDS

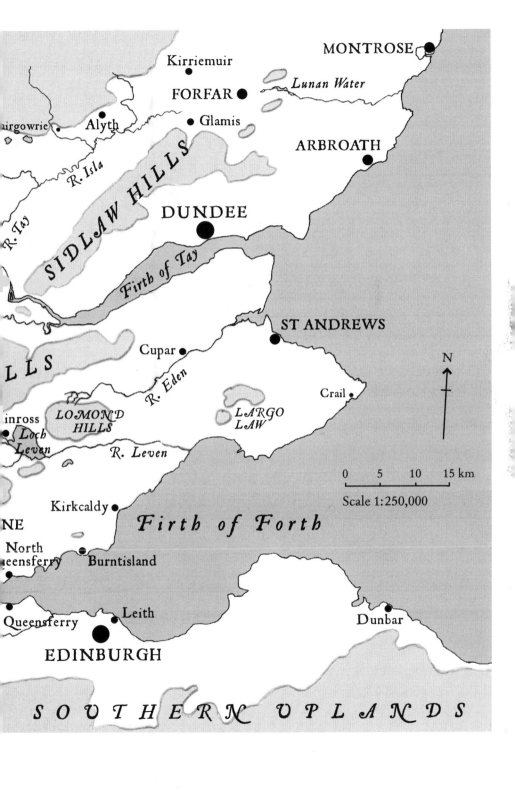

Chapter 1

TWO PARTIES: THE ORIGINS OF JACOBITISM

T O UNDERSTAND how the political situation in Scotland had become so polarised by 1715, we have to go back to the Protestant Reformation of the sixteenth century. The Reformation was not a single event and it played out differently in different countries. In Scotland, it was revolutionary, complex, and prolonged, and St John's Kirk of Perth was the site of some important events. St John's is one of the few buildings in Perth that predates the Jacobite era. The church as we see it today, with its tower and spire, largely dates from the fifteenth century. Although it has been altered both internally and externally over the years, it is still a conspicuous landmark (*see* FIGURE 1). For centuries it was the only church in Perth, which in old documents is often referred to as 'Saint Johns toun' (sometimes St John's Toun or St Johnstoun.)

In May 1559, John Knox preached an inflammatory sermon in St John's, denouncing what he called the 'idolatory' of the Catholic church. This sparked off one of the first violent events of the Scottish Reformation, when crowds not only stripped the altars of St John's but went on to sack and destroy the four great monastic foundations of Perth. The Scottish crown expropriated much of the wealth that had previously maintained religious establishments. Church land was feued (leased in perpetuity), much of it to existing landowners (known as heritors in Scotland). This increased the prosperity of heritors while leaving the reformed church without an adequate source of income. St John's Kirk had originally belonged to Dunfermline Abbey, receiving an income from the abbey's lands, but after the Reformation it became the responsibility of the Perth burgh council.

Prospectus Civitatis PERTHI . G

FIGURE I. *'The Prospect of ye Town of Perth'*. This engraving, dating from 1693, shows St John's Kirk at the centre of the town. Perth is seen from the east bank of the River Tay.

3

The change of religious practice required changes to the fabric of the church. The Latin mass had normally lasted perhaps half an hour, short enough for people to stand, or even walk around the church, while the priest recited the Latin liturgy, which the congregation did not understand and did not really listen to. In a Protestant service, by contrast, preaching from the pulpit became the focus of attention. The congregation was expected to listen attentively to lengthy prayers and sermons, perhaps even take notes. The whole service might last two or three hours, so seating had to be installed.

By 1595, St John's was running out of space as Perth's population grew. The town appointed a second minister (the 'second charge') and the large congregation was divided in two. The nave of the kirk was walled off to form the West Kirk, the transepts and crossing became the East Kirk, and galleries were built to increase the seating capacity. The choir area at the east end was left empty.

The Scottish Reformation had begun as a conflict between Catholicism and the Reformed faith, but it quickly became a struggle for power between King James VI and the new church, which considered itself to be independent of the monarchy. The traditional hierarchy of bishops was still in place, coexisting uneasily with the new presbyteries and synods. Episcopacy was a top-down, centralised type of governance by bishops and archbishops who had a role in government and were appointed by the sovereign. Presbyterian church government did not need the hierarchy of bishops and archbishops: each parish church was run by its kirk session, a committee made up of the minister and lay elders. The kirk session had the power to appoint and dismiss the parish minister, superseding the traditional practice where the minister was chosen by a local landowner. In post-Reformation Scotland the minister had considerable power to discipline his parishioners, and installing a man who supported the patron's own views was an important element of social control. The loss of this right of patronage was greatly resented by the social elites.

The Scottish parliament formally adopted the Presbyterian system in 1592, but James VI was not happy with it despite being brought up in the Reformed faith. Between 1585 and 1600, vacant Scottish bishoprics were not filled, but in 1600 James appointed bishops to represent the church in the Scottish parliament. James was deeply concerned about the theological basis of government and believed that kings ruled by divine right. This meant that the king was not subject to earthly authority: he ruled by the grace of God, and any attempt to dethrone him could be considered sacrilege. Later Stuart kings would inherit this political theory, which inevitably caused them to clash with the secular power of parliament.

The death of Queen Elizabeth I led to the Union of the Crowns of Scotland and England. In 1603, James VI and I, as he now was, moved to London. Since Henry VIII's split from Rome, the English monarch had been head of the Anglican church. When James came to England, he was impressed by how the church hierarchy centralised power in royal hands, and in 1610 he reintroduced diocesan bishops to Scotland. The powers of these bishops were more restricted than those of their English counterparts as they still had to work within the Presbyterian system. Church services continued to follow Presbyterian practice and kirk sessions retained their powers. Toleration, or any idea of 'live and let live', was feared as a slippery slope: freedom of religion might lead to chaos and damnation. Ministers kept a very close eye on their parishioners, and discipline was strict.

In 1618, James forced further changes to bring the Presbyterian practices of the Scottish kirk closer to the Episcopalian pattern of the Anglican church. Introduced at a general assembly held in St John's Kirk in Perth, these innovations became known as the Five Articles of Perth. They concerned kneeling to take communion; private communion (for the sick, for example); infant baptism; confirmation by a bishop; and observance of holy days such as Christmas and Easter. The Reformed church in Scotland had abandoned these practices because they believed that kneeling at communion was too like the Catholic mass; that baptism and confirmation were unnecessary; and that holy days should not be celebrated because they were not mentioned in the Bible. Initially there was widespread resistance to the changes, but the king made it clear that he expected obedience. The Five Articles were eventually accepted by the Scottish parliament in 1621 and became the law of the land. Although John Malcolm, the minister of St John's Kirk at the time, had earlier objected to the reintroduction of episcopacy, the Perth kirk session records for 5 March 1619 report that 'all agreed in one that the celebration thereof be made according to the said Act' (i.e. the congregation should kneel to take communion).

Many ministers and lay people deeply resented the king's reintroduction of bishops and the changes he imposed: others welcomed them. Although there were no formal denominations in the seventeenth-century Scottish church, there was already a rift between Presbyterian and Episcopalian tendencies. The main difference was not what people believed, but what system of church governance they supported. For most of the century, the hierarchy of bishops existed alongside kirk sessions and presbyteries. Inevitably there was a power struggle between the two systems, and church governance was always near the top of the political agenda.

The struggle between Episcopalian and Presbyterian factions of the church continued into the reign of James VI and I's son, Charles I. Encouraged by William Laud, the Archbishop of Canterbury, Charles tried to introduce a prayer book for use in Scotland, similar to the Book of Common Prayer used in England. When it was first used at St Giles' Cathedral in Edinburgh in 1637, tradition has it that a market-woman, Jenny Geddes, threw a stool at the clergyman's head and shouted abuse. This act is reputed to have sparked the riot that led to the Wars of the Three Kingdoms, a series of civil wars in Scotland, England, and Ireland between 1639 and 1651.

In 1638, a National Covenant was signed; this was a document denouncing the Pope and the Catholic church and pledging Scotland to uphold the Reformed religion. Since the previous century there had been several versions of the covenant, and there would be more to come, but the 1638 version is the best known because it was widely circulated, with copies sent around the country for signing. The Perth kirk session renounced Episcopalianism and returned to its previous Presbyterian practices, once again abolishing Christmas and the rest of the Five Articles. Church governance remained Presbyterian through the civil wars of the 1640s and the Cromwellian occupation of the 1650s.

After his Restoration in 1660, King Charles II, son of the executed Charles I, reinstated the bishops. This move was more popular in England than in Scotland. Under the Restoration settlement, refusal to conform to the established church was regarded as treason against the king.

Between 1660 and 1689, Presbyterians attending unauthorised services (known as conventicles), in the open air or in a private house, were breaking the law. If they were discovered, 'conventiclers' were arrested and handed over to local magistrates to be dealt with, often very harshly, by the criminal law. The lucky ones escaped with a heavy fine. The period between 1680 and 1688, when the persecution was at its worst, was later described by Presbyterian historians as the 'killing time'. Preaching at a conventicle was a capital offence, and there were around a hundred executions. Torture was used to compel prisoners to admit the names of their fellow-worshippers. Violence was not all on the government side: James Sharp, the archbishop of St Andrews, was assassinated by extremist Covenanters in 1679. Sharp was particularly unpopular with the Covenanters because he was seen as a traitor to the Kirk; originally a Presbyterian minister, he had changed sides.

Perhaps thanks to the popularity of Sir Walter Scott's *Old Mortality* the Covenanters are generally associated with Glasgow and the southwest of Scotland, but Perthshire was not spared. In the 1680s, Perth's provost Patrick Threipland received thanks from the Chancellor and a knighthood, and later a baronetcy, for his diligence in punishing the keepers of conventicles. Sheriff-Depute John Ramsay was later remembered 'for his cruelty in distressing those whose consciences would not allow them to conform and attend the Kirk' during that time.

In October 1678, Anne Keith, wife of the laird of Methven, took a robust approach to dispersing a conventicle. At a time when her husband, Patrick Smyth, was away in London, a large group of conventiclers, including many citizens of Perth, assembled on the Methven estate (about seven miles west of the town). Lady Methven, armed with a sword and a pistol, rode out at the head of about sixty followers and dependants, and told them that 'unless they left her husband's grounds, it should be a bloody day'. The conventiclers were eventually persuaded to move off the estate and did not return. It is clear from Lady Methven's letters to her husband describing these events that she was a staunch Episcopalian, but religion was not her only reason for seeing off the conventiclers. If they had been known to use the Methven estate as a meeting place, the laird's family could have been accused of helping or harbouring them, a serious offence in itself.

Charles II died in 1685. As he had no legitimate children, his younger brother James, Duke of York, was his heir. James had converted to Catholicism, and many people (who came to be known as Whigs) believed that this ought to bar him from succeeding to the throne. To get him out of London when this controversy was at its height, Charles appointed James as his Lord High Commissioner of Scotland. He spent three years in Edinburgh, from 1679 to 1682, and despite his Catholicism Edinburgh society welcomed a royal presence at Holyrood Palace that had been absent since 1603. The Duke of York attracted many courtiers and extended royal patronage to Scottish institutions such as the College of Physicians and the Advocates Library. He also brought his younger daughter Anne to Edinburgh for a stay of several months in 1681 and 1682, when she would have been just sixteen. Unlike William and Mary (her predecessors on the throne) and the first three Georges who succeeded her, Anne at least had this brief experience of life in Scotland.

The Duke of York is often blamed for the harsh prosecution of Covenanters in the 1680s, but in fact his approach seems to have been relatively humane: he advised the Scottish bishops to ignore conventicles in private houses. When he succeeded as King James II (James VII and II in Scotland) in 1685, the Scottish government was effectively run for him by James Drummond, the fourth Earl of Perth, and his brother Lord Melfort. Perth was Lord Chancellor of Scotland, based in Edinburgh, and Melfort was joint Secretary of State, based in London. The brothers were both recent Catholic converts, and although their conversions may have been sincere, they were understandably viewed as opportunistic. James II used his royal prerogative to appoint Catholics as army commanders and court officials. This policy of so-called 'toleration' extended to Catholics but not to Presbyterians and was deeply unpopular in Scotland.

Historians' accounts of the Glorious Revolution of 1688 vary so widely that it is hard to believe they are all describing the same events. Either James II or William of Orange can be cast as the saviour of the nation or as a complete villain. William indisputably landed in England with a considerable army, while protesting that he did not want to take the crown himself and was merely attempting to prevent James II from causing further harm with his pro-Catholic measures, and to ensure that Britain added its strength to the struggle against the king of France, Louis XIV. Can this be true? If so, when did he change his mind and agree to accept the throne? We do not know.

What we do know is that the conspiracy and undercover dealings that brought William and his troops to England happened south of the border. Once James II fled to France in December 1688, the Scots were presented with a fait accompli. Scottish magnates, including Bishop Rose of Edinburgh, hastily went to London to find out what the consequences would be for themselves and their country. They agreed with William to call a parliament: the so-called Convention Parliament, the only one William ever called in Scotland, first met in March 1689. The Convention Parliament voted overwhelmingly to accept William as king, although on rather different terms from the English parliament. James was deemed to have 'forefaulted' (forfeited) the throne of Scotland, rather than abdicated.

At the time the Convention Parliament met, James II was at the head of a Catholic army in Ireland and there was a real fear that he might invade Scotland, bringing men to join John Graham of Claverhouse, later Viscount Dundee (*see* CHAPTER 2). Loyalty to the Stuart dynasty had been greatly strained by the policies of James II and the men who managed his affairs in Scotland: Lord Perth and Lord Melfort. Both brothers went into exile with James II when he fled to France in 1688. As Catholic converts, the brothers were objects of suspicion, especially to Presbyterians. On their estates in Perthshire – Drummond Castle, near Crieff, and Stobhall, just a few miles north of Perth – they had private chapels where Catholic priests officiated.

Royal burghs like Perth had over the centuries become self-governing oligarchies that resented interference with their internal affairs, but James II and his ministers exerted undue influence in local politics. In Perth from 1686 to 1688, for example, local elections were declared void, and elected officials were replaced by the Privy Council's nominees. In February 1689, an argument arose when Bailie Henry Deas insisted that all town councillors should swear that they were 'true Protestants conform to the Prince of Orange's declaration'. Bailie Deas accused James Stewart, who had been appointed dean of guild by the Privy Council in 1687, of being 'frequently at the Popish worship, particularly in summer last at Stobhall', and of having been introduced to James II in London by a Catholic priest. Stewart 'menaced, threatened, and abused the Provost and Bailie Deas', and the meeting seems to have ended in confusion. The suspicion that James's Privy Council had introduced a crypto-Catholic official into the town council would have horrified the burgesses of Perth, but while James II was still on the throne they would not have felt able to object.

In Scotland, the Revolution of 1689 that brought William of Orange and his wife, James II's elder daughter Mary, to the throne was especially welcomed by Whigs and perceived as a relief from tyranny, but it was not 'glorious', or bloodless. William had been brought up in the Reformed religion, but like his Stuart predecessors he recognised the value of Episcopalian church governance as an instrument of discipline and social control. Most of the English bishops were willing to accept William as their king, in fact if not in law; the minority who did not were known as non-jurors because they would not swear an oath of allegiance to the new king. William expected the Scottish bishops to be equally amenable. Their sole representative in London in January 1689 was Alexander Rose, the bishop of Edinburgh, who had been the minister of St John's Kirk (1678–83), and had married the daughter of Sir Patrick Threipland, provost of Perth at that time. Choosing his words carefully, Rose told William that the Scottish bishops would serve him as far as 'law, reason or conscience' would allow. William correctly understood this as meaning that the bishops would maintain their allegiance to James II: although they wanted William's protection against hostility from the Whigs, they were not willing to accept him as their rightful king. A few months later, William abolished the Scottish episcopate, making the established church in Scotland Presbyterian again.

This was the fourth time in a century that the governance of the Scottish church had been reversed by royal decree or political pressure, and it was to be the last. From then on, the established church in Scotland would remain Presbyterian, while the Episcopalians would gradually build a church in their own tradition. Stuart rule had favoured the Episcopalians, and after the Revolution it was natural for them to look back to the way things had been under Charles II and even James II. Equally naturally, Presbyterians looked forward to restoring the Kirk to what they saw as its original Reformed purity. After a century of conflict and armed struggle these had become political as well as religious worldviews. In September 1715, the difference between the two factions broke out into open rebellion. According to George Farquhar, a nineteenth-century Episcopalian historian, many Episcopalians took up the Jacobite cause because their loyalty to the Stuarts 'had been raised to white heat by the persecution, which they had lately been compelled to endure at the hands of their rivals'.

It is one thing to espouse the Jacobite cause and another thing to take up arms, but to quote the present-day historian Daniel Szechi, 'in the early modern era only religion could justify killing and maiming one's neighbours, friends and kinsmen'. It is impossible to overstate the role of religion in all aspects of life in early modern Scotland. Religious faith is a private matter, but religious observance is public. In a society where non-conformity is punishable, refusal to conform is an obvious badge of identity and becomes a matter of record. In the quarter-century between the Revolution of 1690 and the 1715 rebellion, the worldly issues discussed in the next chapter would further deepen the divide. As the eminent Scottish historian Bruce Lenman puts it, 'there were two parties virtually everywhere in Scotland in 1715'.

Chapter 2

KING WILLIAM'S
'ILL YEARS'

WILLIAM OF ORANGE took the throne as William III of England (William II of Scotland). William had Stuart blood: he was James II's nephew, as his mother was the daughter of Charles I. Although nominally he ruled jointly with his wife Mary, the elder daughter of James II, he made it clear from the beginning that he was in charge.

One man who remained loyal to James II after he was deposed was the Scottish professional soldier John Graham of Claverhouse. He knew both William of Orange and James II personally: he had served under William in the Dutch wars and was part of James's court circle both in Edinburgh when James II was still Duke of York, and later in London.

In 1678, Claverhouse was given command of troops policing religious unrest, in other words suppressing Presbyterian conventicles. He became much feared and hated in the south-west of Scotland, his main area of operation. Claverhouse encouraged James to resist William's invasion in 1688. Before fleeing to France, James created him Viscount Dundee and promoted him to be commander-in-chief of all Scottish forces. In 1689, he was declared a rebel by the Scottish parliament in Edinburgh, with a price on his head. He rallied some support from the Highland clans and hoped that James II, who was then campaigning in Ireland, would either come to Scotland or send him troops, but no help came.

In May 1689, Claverhouse raided Perth, dispersing two newly raised troops of cavalry, seizing some of their horses, taking two of their officers prisoner, and removing 9,000 merks (£6,000 Scots) of tax revenues from the burgh treasury. He declared that he saw nothing wrong in appropriating the king's money for the king's (i.e. James II's) service. At its best his army probably numbered fewer than 2,000 men, but this was enough to overcome government troops at Killiecrankie in July 1689, although Claverhouse himself was killed late in the action. His victorious little army was demoralised by his death; a few weeks later, the government army defeated the remnants of them at Dunkeld.

Claverhouse's rising sparked off clan warfare throughout the Highlands for the next three years, although this may have owed as much to traditional local rivalries as to national politics. However, William and his government were rightly blamed for the 1692 massacre of Glencoe, which soon became a propaganda gift for the anti-Williamites.

Claverhouse seems to have been prompted by genuine loyalty to James II, but he attracted little support from anyone with real power. After his death, Claverhouse was execrated as 'Bluidy Clavers' for his pursuit and harassment of conventiclers but celebrated as 'Bonnie Dundee' for his brave Jacobite exploits. That two such antithetical epithets could be applied to the same man provides an insight into the deep religio-political divisions in Scotland at that time.

A few years of careful kingship might have reconciled most Scots to William's rule, but this was not to happen. For William, Scotland was an annoying encumbrance, although a useful source of the soldiers he needed for his war against Louis XIV. He never visited the country and is reputed to have told the Duke of Hamilton 'I only wish that Scotland was a hundred thousand miles off; and that you were king of it!'

Since medieval times, the Low Countries (modern Belgium and the Netherlands) had been Scotland's main overseas trading partner, with a staple port at Veere at the mouth of the Rhine. The Anglo-Dutch wars of the seventeenth century had a devastating effect on Scotland's trade, especially the east-coast ports. The advent of William meant there would be no more wars with the Dutch, but in 1696 the English parliament passed a Navigation Act that barred Scottish vessels from trading with the American plantations. This trade promptly went underground: the smuggling of tobacco to ports on the west coast of Scotland and then into England became highly lucrative. Smuggling of luxury goods from the continent was rife on the east coast too. The Scots were not accustomed to much vigilance from their customs officials, who were not government men but local appointees who could usually be persuaded to turn a blind eye.

In the 1690s, much of northern Europe, including Scotland, endured several years of bad harvests that caused scarcity and famine. The harvest failures were caused by bad weather, even worse than usual for this period, which is known as the Little Ice Age. Higher, poorer land that could be cultivated in better times could no longer support the local population, who were forced to beg for food in the towns. Even in areas of good agricultural land, such as lowland Perthshire, harvest yields fell. The price of grain (set by burgh councils) rose steeply and in some years there were food riots. Parish records of births and deaths are patchy at best during these years of religious conflict, but the mortality rate in the 1690s was certainly high. It was normal at that time to see such natural disasters as God's punishment for misdeeds, so it was easy for those who resented William to see them as signs that things had gone sadly wrong in Scotland since 1689, blaming him for the 'Ill Years'.

Landowners lived on their tenants' rents, in cash and in kind. The agricultural depression of the 1690s would have affected their income, perhaps making them more willing to invest in the Company of Scotland Trading to Africa and the Indies, now usually known as the Darien scheme. This attempt to found a trading post and colony on the coast of Panama – not Africa, despite the company's name – was a poorly conceived and overambitious project and its failure was probably inevitable, but many Scots resented the English government's hostility to the scheme and its unwillingness to help the distressed colonists. The town council of Perth invested £2,000 of the town's money in the Company, and several individuals from Perth and Perthshire also subscribed. Some were landowners, like James Oliphant of Gask; others were prosperous burgesses, like John Paterson of Craigie, merchants Andrew Gardiner and John Threipland, and the medical men James Murray and William Stewart. The investors lost their money when the scheme collapsed in 1700, although they eventually received compensation after the Union.

After William's abolition of the Scottish episcopate in 1690, the re-established Presbyterian church soon began to stretch its muscles.

Episcopalian clergymen, or anyone attending unauthorised services, could be harassed by the local kirk session or presbytery. However, physically ejecting an Episcopalian incumbent and gaining possession of his parish church and manse (the minister's house) required the aid of the secular arm – the sheriff and his deputies, who were usually drawn from the ranks of local elites. In Perthshire and further north, many heritor families had Episcopalian sympathies and the head of the family was often the traditional patron of the local church. They might be unwilling to enforce the local presbytery's ruling, even when it was backed up by the Privy Council in Edinburgh. Sheriff-Depute John Ramsay, who was the son of an Episcopalian minister, simply refused the Perth Presbytery's request to take part in the deprivation of the Episcopalian incumbent at Cargill in 1703. Social pressure and delaying tactics were so effective that it could take years for a Presbyterian minister to gain access to the parish church and the manse.

It was one thing for the Scottish parliament to pass a law (the Confession of Faith Ratification Act 1690) and another thing to impose a change of denomination in every parish throughout the country. As a Presbyterian historian, James Scott (minister of St John's 1771–1807), writes,

> [N]ot only the nobility and gentry, but also the bulk of the people, were fondly attached to the Episcopal incumbents. In the Presbytery of Perth, such ministers as had given greatest offence by their disaffection to the new Government were deprived very early, not with the minds of the people, but contrary thereto ... [I]t was no easy matter to prevail afterwards with most of these parishes to accept of Presbyterian ministers.

As well as a lack of popular will, there was a shortage of Presbyterian ministers in a country that had been nominally Episcopalian for a generation. Hard as it was to dislodge an Episcopalian incumbent, it was even harder to find a suitable replacement. In many Perthshire parishes, Presbyterian ministers were not finally installed until well into the eighteenth century.

The Episcopalians began to set up their own places of worship, known as meeting-houses. This separation of congregations marks the beginning of what is now the Episcopal Church of Scotland. The bishops, although dismissed from their official positions in 1690, had never gone away and they continued their pastoral role. In Perth, the Episcopalian congregation had asked if they could hold their services in the east end of St John's Kirk, which remained unused, but the kirk session did not allow it. At one time they rented a room in Parliament Close, off the High Street (on the present site of Marks & Spencer), but other sites, now untraceable, may also have been used.

In seventeenth-century Scotland, the practice was for prayers to be extempore, not read from a book. The reading of prayers had caused a riot in St Giles' Cathedral in Edinburgh in 1637, and no attempt had been made to introduce a Scottish prayer book since then. In 1709, the Perth Presbytery objected to Episcopalian clergymen, including William Smyth, the former incumbent of the Perthshire parish of Moneydie, using the English prayer book. They condemned this as an 'innovation'. Mr Smyth was also accused of conducting a burial service using a service book while wearing a black gown. This, according to the Presbytery, was 'of most dangerous consequence, as manifestly tending to grieve the godly, lay a stumbling-block before the weak, and to harden Papists in their superstition'. William Smyth was now quite an elderly man, and his son James spoke on his father's behalf in the Presbytery's proceedings. James Smyth was a surgeon and apothecary in Perth who was named in Hay's commission to take the town in 1715 and served as a bailie (i.e. a magistrate) on the Jacobite town council. During the Battle of Sheriffmuir, James Smyth reverted to his earlier role as an army surgeon.

The excessive zeal of the Perth Presbytery in pursuing Episcopalian incumbents probably helped to ensure the passage of the Scottish Episcopalians Act 1711, otherwise known as the Toleration Act. Its full title is 'An Act to prevent the disturbing those of the Episcopal Communion in Scotland in the Exercise of their Religious Worship and in the Use of the Liturgy of the Church of England and for repealing the Act passed in the Parliament of Scotland intituled Act against irregular Baptisms and Marriages'. Although few if any Episcopalian ministers ever took the anti-Jacobite oath required by the Act, they were, nevertheless, able to serve their congregations in the way the

Presbytery had been harassing them about since 1690. In the same year, parliament passed 'An Act to restore the Patrons to their ancient Rights of presenting Ministers to the Churches vacant in that part of Great Britain called Scotland'. This returned power to landowners and town councils to nominate ministers, rather than congregations having the right to call a minister of their choice. One can almost hear the gnashing of Presbyterian teeth.

By 1715, the Perth Presbytery evidently thought they had done enough. When asked to make a collection for 'defraying the expenses the Church has been at in commencing processes for removing intruders into Churches and suppressing other Disorders', they refused to contribute, 'having been at great charges already in processing Episcopal Incumbents and getting them removed, and planting of Churches in their bounds since the late happy Revolution, without any reparation'.

The Presbytery also objected to the setting up of Episcopalian meeting-houses by clergymen deprived of their livings, whom they described (rather illogically) as 'intruders'. Complaints about the meeting-house in Perth dragged on for years, and in 1699 the Presbytery asked the provost for help in suppressing it. The provost at the time was Patrick Davidson, who would later head the Jacobite town council of 1715–16. He told the Presbytery he was 'loth to meddle', although he allowed them to examine witnesses about attendance at Episcopalian services. One such witness was Joseph Taylor, who was to be a Jacobite activist in 1715. In 1706, Sheriff-Depute Ramsay refused a further request from the Presbytery to suppress the Perth meeting-house.

It is widely believed that many Scottish Jacobites were Catholic, but this is a misapprehension. At that time, Catholics formed a very small minority of the population of Scotland. Both Episcopalians and Presbyterians were staunch Protestants who would have described themselves as anti-Papist. It is true that James II, his son, and his grandson ('Bonnie Prince Charlie') were Catholics, and so were many members of the later Jacobite diaspora, but although there were some important exceptions, such as the Drummond brothers, almost all the active Jacobites in Scotland in 1715 were Episcopalian. This can readily be traced in the Perth records. In 1705, George Threipland, George Wilson, and

John Gourlay admitted to the kirk session that they had been married to their wives by an Episcopalian minister. All three were to be active in the 1715 rising: Gourlay became the burgh treasurer during the Jacobite occupation; Threipland was held prisoner and was in danger of being sent to Carlisle in 1716; Wilson became a member of the Jacobite town council, served as an ensign in one of the town's companies, and was on the 1718 list of banished rebels. Other Perth men who attended Episcopalian services, in addition to Joseph Taylor, who was a hammerman (i.e. a metalworker; he is sometimes described as a cutler), were Mark Wood, merchant; Nathaniel Fyffe, merchant; John Simson, cooper; David Walker, late deacon convener; Patrick Richie, bellman (i.e. verger or sexton); Charles Wilson, sometime deacon of the glovers; and John Alexander, grave maker. Deacons were important men, elected officials of the craft guilds, so this was quite a cross-section of Perth society.

What proportion of the population of Perth was Presbyterian by preference by 1715 is unknown. The two Episcopalian ministers of St John's Kirk had been deprived of their livings in 1689, but many local people – again, we do not know how many – remained loyal to their Episcopalian beliefs. This religious disagreement was mirrored by a political divide. We can call the two parties Whig and Jacobite (or Tory) for convenience, always bearing in mind their religious underpinnings. Neither party thought the Union of 1707 was a success, but it was the Jacobites who were able to take advantage of anti-Union sentiment by offering an alternative to King George I.

In 1715, the senior minister of St John's Kirk was Thomas Black, who had been appointed Professor of Divinity at St Andrews by Queen Anne in September 1707 but retained his parochial charge until his death in 1741. He was elected Moderator of the General Assembly in 1721. The minister of the second charge was John Fleming and in 1716 the town council appointed William Wilson to a third charge. From 1703 until 1716, the Episcopalian incumbent at Perth's meeting-house was Henry Murray. He left Perth in 1716 after the failure of the rising and had returned, with Laurence Drummond as his assistant, by 1722, although there are records of other Episcopalian clergymen officiating covertly in or near Perth before that. A law passed in 1719 forbade Episcopalian clergy to hold services unless they took an oath of loyalty to George I, but Murray seems to have somehow avoided this: apparently he was 'in the habit of praying for her Majesty [Queen Anne], but after her death never complying nor praying for the King [George I]'.

The 1701 Act of Settlement specified that after Anne's death the crown of England was to go to the Hanoverians, passing over dozens of Catholic Stuart cousins to their closest Protestant relatives. The Scottish parliament had not passed such an act and was unwilling to do so. In 1703, it passed An Act for Security of the Kingdom, specifying that

> ... it shall not be in the power of the said meeting of estates to name the successor of the crown of England to be successor to the imperial crown of this realm, nor shall the same person be capable, in any event, to be king or queen of both realms, unless a free comm-unication of trade, the freedom of navigation and the liberty of plantations be fully agreed to and established by the parliament and kingdom of England to the kingdom and subjects of Scotland. ...

Unless England accepted the free trade provisions, which parliament had never been willing to do, this would have abolished the 1603 Union of the Crowns and left the door open for a Stuart restoration.

The English parliament responded with the 1705 Alien Act, declaring that Scottish nationals in England were to be treated as aliens and that estates in England held by Scots would be treated as alien property, meaning that English laws of inheritance would not apply. Far from encouraging free trade between England and Scotland, the Alien Act prohibited the import of Scottish products into England and the English colonies in North America, including major exports such as linen, cattle, and coal. However, the Act contained a provision that it would be suspended if the Scots entered into negotiations regarding a proposed union of the parliaments of Scotland and England. At the same time, offers were made to refund Scottish losses on the Darien scheme, for which the Scots had been quick to lay the blame on England. This carrot-and-stick approach soon achieved its aim: negotiations began in 1706, leading to the Acts of Union 1707 uniting England and Scotland as the Kingdom of Great Britain.

It is important to see this quarrel between England and Scotland in a wider European context. Since 1688, with only a brief hiatus from 1697 to 1701, the whole continent had been at war. The Nine Years' War (1688–97) was followed by the War of the Spanish Succession (1701–14). England was part of a Grand Alliance with the Dutch Republic and the Austrian empire, fighting against France. One thing Protestants both in Scotland and in England could agree on was that they were anti-Catholic. They feared the powerful combination of Catholicism, absolute monarchy, and religious persecution and they had an example of this close at hand, in the France of Louis XIV. Louis had been on the throne for longer than most people could remember, from 1643 (at the age of four) until his death in 1715.

The French king was an apparently permanent feature at a time when monarchy in Britain was in turmoil: execution of a king, abolition of the monarchy, the Restoration, the Revolution of 1689. Louis, the Sun King, centralised power in his court at Versailles and expanded royal authority at the expense of the aristocracy's traditional privileges. War, to increase French unity at home and its power throughout Europe, was an important part of his strategy and self-image. In his reign, France became a military superpower. It also became an unsafe place for Protestants. In the 1598 Edict of Nantes, Louis's grandfather Henri IV had granted political and religious freedom to French Protestants, known as Huguenots. Louis, on the other hand, believed that he should be able to decree what religion his subjects followed. The concept that the religion of the ruler should be the religion of those he ruled, epitomised in the Latin motto *cuius regio, eius religio*, was not new; it had been followed throughout Europe, including Britain, since the Reformation. But Louis's attempt to abolish Protestantism was particularly brutal, and Huguenot refugees fleeing persecution gave horrific accounts of what they had suffered, both before and after the Edict of Nantes was revoked in 1685. It was taken as a grim warning of what might happen if Louis ever invaded Britain.

When William III died in 1702, Queen Anne inherited a state of war. Anne had spent part of her early childhood in France under the care of her grandmother Henrietta Maria, and she spoke and wrote French well. She may not have felt any personal antipathy to France, but in her first speech to parliament she stated that she was 'entirely English' and would not change William's domestic or international policies.

Eighteenth-century wars such as the War of the Spanish Succession were fought by huge armies that covered great distances, posing great financial and logistical problems for the combatants. Over 100,000 men, many of whom had marched halfway across Europe, fought at the Battle of Blenheim in 1704, and other battles were on a similarly gargantuan scale. Blenheim was a great victory for the Duke of Marlborough and his allied forces. The French suffered a crushing defeat that was decisive for the eventual outcome of the war, although hostilities were to continue for a further decade and many more thousands of soldiers would die. The idea that Scotland could somehow offer Louis XIV's armies a way to attack England by reviving the 'auld alliance' with France was intolerable to the English government, and the legislative stand-off between the separate parliaments could not be allowed to continue. Some Scots would have favoured a looser, federal type of arrangement, but the English insisted on an incorporating Union to avoid any possibility of Scotland having an independent foreign policy.

For Scots, the pro-Unionist argument was that the Union would maintain the revolution of 1689 and the Protestant religion and would secure the future economic prosperity of Scotland. The majority of Scots did not believe this and did not want the Union; there were riots against it in Glasgow and other towns. To begin with, the Scottish kirk opposed the Union, fearing the return of episcopacy, but the English negotiators were content to allow the Scots to keep their Presbyterian kirk (despite some Tory fears that this would be a threat to the English church), as well as their own legal system. The overwhelming English interest was to maintain its own national security, the Union of the Crowns, and the Protestant succession, which inevitably made the Union an anti-Jacobite measure.

Protests against the Union came from many quarters, Whig as well as Jacobite, including the town councils of Perth and many other burghs as well as their centuries-old representative body, the Convention of Royal Burghs, which normally had considerable influence on the Scottish parliament. The Convention's petition expressed many of the Scottish objections to an incorporating Union:

by which our Monarchy is supprest, our Parliament is extinguished and in consequence our Religion, Church, Government, Claim of Right, Laws, Liberties, Trade and all that is dear to us daily in danger of being encroached upon, altered or wholly subverted by the English, in a British Parliament, wherein the mean representation allowed for Scotland can never signify in securing to us the Interest reserved by us, or granted to us by the English.

Perth's own petition repeated all the general points about sovereignty and the church but added some that were more specific to the burgh. The council feared that the Union would

put trade, the great interest of the burgh, under the heaviest burdens, taxes, and impositions without any Parliament to hear and help us, except that of the British one whose interest as we may perceive will never dispose them to favour our prosperity where they can pretend but an imaginary loss by our gain.

The county of Perthshire had also presented an anti-Unionist address, although their petition omitted the usual fears that the Union might weaken the position of the Scottish kirk, a reflection of the strength of Episcopalianism in the county.

The Scottish parliament paid no attention to the petitions; the Duke of Argyll is said to have called them 'paper kites'. The franchise in Scotland was minuscule, only about two per cent of the population, and public opinion was not an important factor in political calculations. Many pro-Union votes were secured by offers of well-paid government posts and payment of arrears of salary (a cunning way to bribe people by only paying them what they were already owed), and the Scottish parliament voted in favour of the Treaty of Union by a comfortable majority.

One member who voted against the Treaty of Union was Alexander Robertson of Craig, who had represented Perth since 1702. He had been a town councillor for many years and served as provost in 1705. The two members for Perthshire - John Haldane of Gleneagles and Mungo Graham of Gorthy – were both members of the Squadrone Volante. This exotically named political grouping, earlier more prosaically known as the 'New Party', was independent of the main Court and Country parties. Haldane and Graham voted with their party in favour of the Union, even though the county had presented an address against it.

Perthshire was considered to be largely the political fiefdom of the Duke of Atholl, the major landholder in the area. Atholl was strongly against an incorporating Union and seems to have been involved in conspiracies to prevent it by force. However, he did not record a vote on the Treaty of Union in January 1707; it seems likely that he was not present in parliament because his first wife was then on her deathbed. The political sympathies of Atholl and his family are ambiguous, to say the least. The duke was a Presbyterian in a largely Episcopalian (and therefore Jacobite) county. He had been a firm supporter of William of Orange in the 1690s but was suspected of being involved in the projected Jacobite invasion of 1708. The Jacobite agent Nathaniel Hooke later reported that Atholl gave him no definite commitment of support, but, nevertheless, the Jacobites at St Germain believed that he might be willing to lead the rising in 1715. In fact, many Jacobites were surprised when Atholl and his second son, Lord James Murray, sided with the government in 1715, although three of his other sons (the Marquess of Tullibardine, Lord George Murray, and Lord Charles Murray) joined the Earl of Mar's Jacobite army in Perth.

The Scottish burghs were right to fear that they would not have a powerful voice in the post-Union Westminster parliament, which had only 45 Scottish seats out of the total 568. In the old unicameral Scottish parliament, with 247 seats, the burgh of Perth had had its own representative, but at Westminster it had only a one-fifth share of one. The new Perth Burghs constituency included five burghs in three different counties: Perth itself, Dundee and Forfar in Angus, and Cupar and St Andrews in Fife. Choosing a man to represent this group of burghs was not easy, partly because Perth and Dundee, the largest of them, had a centuries-long and often acrimonious rivalry. The organisation of elections rotated among the three counties, and the outcome largely depended on who was officiating.

The Scottish MPs who came to Westminster in 1708, the first parliament elected after the Union, were not greatly welcomed and did not make a great impression. Joseph Austin of Kilspindie, a Presbyterian

Whig, was elected to represent Perth Burghs. He was the brother of William Austin, who would be the provost of Perth in 1715. Joseph did not distinguish himself at Westminster, apparently not making any contribution to the proceedings and not achieving anything for his constituents. He did not stand in the 1710 election, and the seat then went to George Yeaman of Dundee, a shipowner and former slave trader, who was an Episcopalian Tory.

Keen to advance the interests of his co-religionists in Scotland, Yeaman voted in favour of the Church Patronage (Scotland) Act of 1711 and the Toleration Act of 1712. Yeaman was a much more active MP than Austin had been and achieved some good results for his constituents (in Perth as well as Dundee), reducing duties on water-borne coal and bringing in a bill to encourage the manufacture of linen in Scotland. By the end of the eighteenth century, the industrialised linen industry would drive the economy of this part of Scotland, but in 1712 it was still a small-scale traditional trade.

Yeaman did not stand for re-election in 1715 and took no further part in public life. Although he may well have had Jacobite sympathies, he conspicuously did not participate in the events of 1715–16. A dispatch from Edinburgh, published in the *St. James's Evening Post* in January 1716, reported that 'Captain Yeaman, Provost of Dundee and formerly Member of Parliament for that Town, on the Preparations being making there for the Pretender's Reception, is retired hither [i.e. to Edinburgh], to avoid being present on that Occasion'.

Patrick Haldane, a Whig who was a professor at St Andrews University, was returned unopposed for Perth Burghs in 1715 (it was Fife's turn to organise the election). In 1716, he was elected provost of St Andrews, allegedly by bribery and intimidation. He was also appointed one of the commissioners for the sale of estates forfeited in the Jacobite rising, with a salary of £1,000. His excessive harshness in dealing with forfeited estates made him unpopular, not only with Jacobites but also with their influential friends and relatives. The Haldane family's estates had been badly damaged by Jacobite raids in 1715 (*see* p.111), and the government had paid only derisory compensation, which may explain his desire to exact retribution.

The county of Perthshire had only one seat at Westminster, rather than the two it had had in Edinburgh. Although many of the landowners who were eligible to vote had Jacobite sympathies, the Atholl Whig interest nevertheless predominated in parliamentary elections. At the first election after the Union in 1708, John Haldane (the father of Patrick) was elected for the Perthshire seat. In 1715, the Duke of Atholl's son, Lord James Murray, was returned and the Perthshire constituency remained in Atholl hands for decades to come.

Before the Union, it had been quite feasible for the provost of Perth to represent the burgh in parliament, as well as in the powerful Convention of Royal Burghs. Edinburgh was only forty miles away, communication was rapid by contemporary standards, and the burgh could afford to pay expenses. London, on the other hand, was almost five hundred miles away, many days' journey for men or letters, and an MP was expected to live there while parliament was sitting. This was expensive, and MPs were not paid a salary. The Perth Burghs constituency is described in the *History of Parliament* as being 'open and venal' at this period, meaning essentially that it elected whoever could afford to buy the most votes in the three counties. This considerable financial commitment and the need to be in London for extended periods ruled out election to parliament for a burgh provost. In Scotland after 1707, local politics and national politics therefore became separate spheres.

Chapter 3

RESTLESS
ENDEAVOURS

I N JUNE 1714, the Perth Presbytery had complained of 'the threatening aspect of affairs ... and the restless endeavours both in Church and State', reflecting the general uneasiness as Queen Anne's reign came to an end. The arrival of King George followed by the Whig landslide victory in the 1715 parliamentary election must have seemed like the last straw for Scottish Jacobites. They had been elbowed out of power in the burghs by the Williamite Revolution of 1689, and the number of parliamentary seats available to them had been slashed by the Union of 1707. Now, a Hanoverian king, a Whig parliament, and Presbyterian burgesses held power, and the Jacobites had no share in it. No wonder they looked back fondly at the days of Charles II and James II and longed for Stuart rule to continue and the Episcopal church to be restored.

Queen Anne, the last reigning Stuart monarch, died on 1 August 1714. She was only forty-nine, but had been in poor health for some time, so her death was not unexpected. None of her children survived her, so under the 1701 Act of Settlement, which excluded all Catholics, she was succeeded by her second cousin George I, the Elector of Hanover.

It is hard not to feel some sympathy for Anne. Her health had never been good, and by the time she was in her mid-thirties she was unable to walk unassisted. Despite at least seventeen pregnancies, she had only one son who survived infancy and he had died in 1700 at the age of eleven. Her husband, Prince George of Denmark, had died in 1708. (Some Jacobites continued to refer to Anne as the Princess of Denmark even after her succession; in their correspondence 'the Queen' is Mary of Modena, the widow of James II.)

It was widely believed at the time, at least by Tories, that Anne was secretly a Jacobite and favoured her half-brother James Francis Edward Stuart, the only legitimate son of James II, to succeed her. There is no evidence of this; quite the opposite, in fact. Anne had been largely responsible for spreading and maintaining the 'warming pan' rumour, that James was a changeling who had been smuggled into Mary of Modena's birthing chamber. Anne publicly and privately supported the Protestant succession, but her policy was to keep a balance between her Whig and Tory ministers. This extended to not showing favour to either Hanoverians or Jacobites, so relations between Anne and the Hanoverians remained distant. The Electress Sophia (George's mother, who died in June 1714) had shown an interest in British politics, which Anne resented, rightly suspecting that any Hanoverian interference was likely to upset the balance she wished to maintain. Anne's refusal to allow any of the Hanoverian family to come to England helped rumours of her Jacobite sympathies to spread.

When they realised that Anne was in decline, the Whigs stirred up anti-Jacobite hysteria in parliament. In June 1714, the ailing queen issued a proclamation offering a £5,000 reward (later increased to £100,000) for the apprehension of James anywhere in England, Scotland, or Ireland. Anne died on the morning of Sunday, 1 August, and the accession of George I was proclaimed the same afternoon. The Tory parliament immediately swore loyalty to the new king and the transition passed off peacefully in all three kingdoms.

In Edinburgh, George I was proclaimed king with great ceremony on 5 August. The town council of Perth formally recorded its allegiance to the Protestant succession. At their first meeting after Anne's death, on 23 August, the councillors swore an oath of allegiance to King George. Joseph Taylor, deacon of the hammermen, refused the oath and was removed from the meeting, although he agreed to swear the oath at the council's next meeting. This was the same Joseph Taylor who had given evidence of his attendance at the Episcopalian meeting-house, and it was not his first refusal to swear an oath of loyalty, as an entry in *The Perth Hammermen Book* recounts:

Patrick Davidson ... advanced 1,000 merks [£666 Scots] to defend a law suit in the Court of Session, raised by the Convener Court to prevent the Deacon of the Hammermen taking his seat in Council, because the year after the Union [1708] he demitted office rather than swear the oath of abjuration [in favour of the Protestant succession].

Evidently Taylor and ex-provost Davidson were on friendly terms, personally or politically, although there would normally have been a social distinction between a tradesman and a prosperous merchant.

King George did not help his own cause by being slow to leave Hanover for England; he did not arrive until 18 September. To many Jacobite sympathisers in England and Scotland, this six-week hiatus seemed like a golden opportunity for James to arrive at the head of an army, but he did not. Why was this? After all, Anne's death had not been unexpected. Could James not have been ready and waiting? As a sarcastic Whig letter-writer later asked, 'Why did they not move in the end of the late reign? Why were they not two months on horsback befor the King [George I] came over?'

Unfortunately for him, James's hands were tied. The 1713 Peace of Utrecht, which ended the War of the Spanish Succession, had been a great blow to Jacobite hopes. The aim of the complex series of military and commercial treaties signed at Utrecht was to maintain the balance of power in Europe, by preventing the union of the crowns of France and Spain. France was exhausted by years of fighting, and Louis XIV was anxious to end the war as soon as possible. He was obliged to accept several conditions that seriously disadvantaged the Jacobites, recognising Anne as queen and accepting the Protestant succession to the British throne. He also agreed that James could no longer live in France. In early 1713, James left the Jacobite court at St Germain for Lorraine, which was then an independent duchy. His mother, Mary of Modena, stayed at St Germain and had her own court there; it remained Jacobite headquarters, still largely supported by Louis XIV.

In Lorraine, James was 250 miles from Paris, cut off from the regular supply of news from Britain that regularly reached St Germain and

Versailles, where the Duke of Berwick had access to the king and to Colbert de Torcy, the foreign secretary. James depended heavily on Berwick, who was his half-brother, to pass on political news and advice. Correspondence was painfully slow and uncertain, and James complained of the 'obscurity and delays' involved. Letters between Lorraine and St Germain or Versailles took at least three days either way, often five or six. To conceal names and sensitive topics in case their letters were intercepted, the Jacobites used what they called 'cipher', or 'cant names'; a form of encryption that required the use of a codebook. It was widely believed at the time that these 'cant names' were more secure than a code, which might be broken – a dubious assumption, as the real names can often be at least guessed at from the context and often had the same initial letter as the cant name.

In February 1715, Berwick wrote to James:

> I beginn to suspect … that Orbec [*the Duke of Ormond*] expects M. Robinson [*James*] should carry with him to M. Elbeuf [*Scotland*] or M. Alencon [*England*] that able lawyer M. Alexandre [*an army*] which at [this] time cannot possibly be compassd …

He was right: although the exiled Jacobites explained that they could not bring a large force of troops with them, the British Jacobites continued to insist this was essential for success. As early as 1710, Charles Leslie, a well-known non-juror clergyman, had written to the court of St Germain:

> Severals in England wish the King [James] well, who would not hazard their estates for him; but these very people would not willingly hazard any thing against him, if they saw the smallest risk on the side of the government. It seems, therefore, that the greatest number want only an opportunity of declaring themselves; that is to say, the return of his Britannic Majesty, with a force sufficient to protect those who would choose to join him on his arrival. If he came with 10,000 men, it is thought there would not be a sword drawn against him; but if he cannot have that number, 5,000 men would render the success probable, but not so certain.

Writing to James in April 1714, Berwick considered what should be done on Queen Anne's death:

> on one side it would look odd in the world that M. Robinson [*James*] should see M. Home [*the Elector of Hanover*] quietly get M. Albert's [*Queen Anne's*] estate [*the throne*] without making the least opposition, on the other side to beginn a law suite [*rebellion*] there must be money, provision of stamped paper [*arms*], and all many other things which I am afeard M. Robinson wants, besides that there can be no hopes of success unless, one can gett some attourneys of M. Alexandre's family [*an army*]: A great many of M. Enster's relations [*the Scots*] will oppose the business, and 'tis much feared M. Moreau [*the Highlanders*] will have but very small meanes for so great an undertaking.

It is an accurate summing up of James's difficulties: no money, no arms, no army, no certainty of how much support he could expect when he arrived.

In June 1714, King Louis ordered Berwick, who was a marshal of the French army, to command his army in Spain. News was slow to reach him there: at the end of August, Berwick was still unaware of Queen Anne's death at the beginning of that month. He was not back in Paris until November. Just at the time when James most needed clear-sighted advice and an ally at the French court, Berwick was not available. However, the situation had not greatly changed since he had so realistically summed it up in April: James was in no position to stage an instant invasion.

Louis XIV had quickly accepted the Hanoverian succession, as the Peace of Utrecht required, and other European powers followed his example. James had set out for Versailles to ask for Louis's help as soon as he heard of Anne's death, but was turned away and told to go back to Lorraine. At the end of August, he issued a 1500-word declaration addressed to 'all Kings, Princes, and Potentates, and our loveing Subjects' and had it distributed to leading members of the nobility in Britain and Europe. The declaration explained his right to the succession, his disappointment that the people of Britain had not taken this recent opportunity to restore him to the throne, and his belief that God would do the right thing in time. James points out that he is 'the only born Englishman now left of the Royall Family' and assures his readers that nothing that had gone wrong was his fault. He concludes that 'in the Circumstances we are in, We have nothing left in our power to do at present'. James was often quick to point out that his misfortunes were not his own fault. His declaration was not a document that would have raised Jacobite spirits, expressing more pathos than political fervour.

In September, James informed his supporters in Scotland that 'no forreign help must be expected at present of men, arms or ammunition'. He dispatched an Irish officer, Sir John Forester, to distribute money (£4,000 sterling, i.e. £48,000 Scots) and information to Jacobites in Scotland. James instructed Forester:

> You will consert with my friends what way the mony sent by you can bee most effectually imployed for my service in buying upp ammunition, or meal, or bringing what arms possibly they may from Hambourgh, Dantzick or any other parts so as to give no jealousy to the present Government.

He also specifies:

> You will particularly ... take and follow the measures approvd of by the B[ishop] of Edinbourgh, whose advice I depend uppon singularly. ...

The Bishop of Edinburgh was Alexander Rose (*see* p.10), now an elderly man. Although William of Orange had deprived the Scottish bishops of their official authority, they had not gone away. By 1715, Rose was the senior non-juring bishop in Scotland, overseeing the embryonic Episcopal church. He would have good pastoral reasons for maintaining correspondence with clergymen throughout Scotland, and with churchmen in England. He had also been in correspondence with the Jacobite court since the Revolution and had written to James to advise him 'not to stirr' at the time of George I's accession. His Jacobite sympathies were no secret and he had come close to being arrested at the time of the attempted invasion in 1708. His correspondence is likely to have been intercepted or watched by government agents, but he would have been able to pass useful information to Forester when they met.

Correspondence could go between France and Scotland either directly or via England. Several agents or intermediaries are mentioned by name in the Stuart correspondence, based in Britain but occasionally travelling to the court at St Germain. They were gentlemen who could easily mingle with elite society without being conspicuous. Captain Henry Stratton, a former Scots Guards officer based in Edinburgh, was the usual means of communication with the chiefs of Highland clans. Colin Campbell of Glendaruel is also named occasionally as a trusted intermediary in the Highlands. The Stuart papers also mention messengers referred to as 'the Highlander' or 'Puckle'. Whether this is just one man or several is not clear, but they (or he) seem to have travelled back and forward to France regularly. These messengers were regarded as servants, lower in the social scale than the named agents.

When Berwick returned from Spain in November 1714, he resumed his role as James's adviser and his conduit to Versailles. On 28 November, he wrote to James, advising him to ask the Scottish Jacobites to be patient:

> In the present situation of affaires all that can be said to the King's [*James's*] friends in Scotland is, That the King is firmly resolved to goe himself in person to them as soon as possibly he can, and to carry me [*Berwick*] along with him. That a little time must be allowed for getting together what is necessary, especially for raising of money and for taking measures with friends in England, without which little good is to be expected. The King is now actually about this.

The last sentence refers to Forester's mission. In early 1715, the Jacobite plan was still for the main focus of the rising to be in the south-west of England, under the leadership of the Duke of Ormonde. A rising in Scotland was to be a secondary affair, a distraction that would divert government troops away from England, but it was a necessary part of the plan, and up-to-date, first-hand information on the state of affairs in Scotland was anxiously awaited. Forester returned in February, with a report that Berwick summarises as 'nothing is yet in a reddiness, nor can be so soon'. Meanwhile, Berwick himself was busy about James's business, with ambitious attempts to source money from the King of Spain to pay for troops from the King of Sweden.

Berwick also did his best to persuade the Duke of Ormonde to come up with firm plans for a rebellion in England, but Ormonde was not 'in a reddiness' either. He had succeeded the Duke of Marlborough as captain-general of the British army, but was dismissed when the Tories fell from favour after the accession of George I. He was a popular and affable man, more generous than his income warranted, with many years of military experience. Although Berwick and James had great faith in him, at least to begin with, he was not the right man to plan an uprising. His replies to Berwick's anxious enquiries were dilatory and vague, and he could not keep secrets. In June 1715, Ormonde was impeached for high treason and in August he fled to France. His main role had been to encourage the nobility and gentry of England to rebel, which he could not do from exile in France. From then on his usefulness to the Jacobite cause was limited. He attempted to lead an expedition to England in October 1715, but this was a complete failure.

Another Tory grandee who had been dismissed from government on George I's accession was Henry St John, Lord Bolingbroke. As one of the major negotiators of the Peace of Utrecht, he was considered by his Whig opponents to have been too favourable to French interests. In March 1715, fearing he was about to be arrested for treason, he fled to France disguised as a servant. His flight was taken as an admission of guilt, which was only confirmed by his appointment as James's secretary of state in July 1715.

After accepting this role, Bolingbroke acted as an archetypal new broom, pointing out shortcomings in the way Jacobite affairs were managed: 'no subordination, no order, no concert', as he wrote to his friend Sir William Wyndham. In particular, he saw that security was slack. Bolingbroke wrote to James that he 'was not a little concerned to hear ... among women over their tea, that arms were provided and ships got ready'. He also assured James that the British government knew all about his invasion plans and cast doubt on the reliability of his spies and messengers. James welcomed his advice:

> I am allways persuaded you will not only not abuse of my confidence, but that my conferring with one who has so great experience will be of advantage to me who have so little and who do my self justice in owning it.

This is typical of James's readiness to depend on an older adviser. As George Lockhart, though a loyal Jacobite, later wrote:

> Nature had made this Prince a quiet unenterprising man, education a bigoted Catholic, and, like most of the Princes of his race, he combined an obstinate and unreasonable pertinacity in what he had once determined, with a blind submission to favourites, sometimes unwisely chosen and always too readily obeyed.

Just as Bolingbroke was taking charge, James and his friends finally received detailed information from the English Jacobites. Charles Kinnaird, one of the trusted Jacobite agents, wrote a note at the end of the document:

> This above written memorial was writ by me and dictated by the Earl of Mar at his house in Whitehall, the 5th of July old style, being Tuesday, and the same day it was carried to Richmond and perused by the Duke of Ormonde and delivered to me by his Grace to carry to the King [James]. He delivered it to me as his instructions in presence of the Earl of Mar and Lord Lansdown.

Mar had been in government office all his adult life, first in Scotland and then after 1707 in England. He had inherited heavily indebted estates and depended on political office for his income. Despite his Scottish Episcopalian background and Tory politics, he had not demonstrated any obvious sympathy for the Jacobite cause before George I's accession. He had written a sycophantic letter promising the new king his support, which George ignored. He seems to have taken up the Jacobite cause simply because he would have no political future, and thus no source of income, under Hanoverian rule.

Having made this decision, Mar was evidently impatient with Ormonde's ineffectiveness. Like the experienced bureaucrat he was, he drafted a business-like memo, more direct in its language than most Jacobite correspondence. He probably realised that he was effectively writing to Bolingbroke, whom he would have known well from their years in office together:

... there is no hope of succeeding in it [the rebellion] without the assistance of a regular force, or without a general raising of the people in all parts of England, immediately upon the King's [James's] landing, and that the latter of these depends very much upon the former. For though the generality of the people are extremely averse from the Court and Ministry (whom they hate and despise) and well inclined to a restoration; yet it is not to be expected that they should declare themselves all at once, unless they see the King attended with such a force as will give some reputation to his undertaking, and encourage the country to come in to him.

Echoing Leslie in 1710, Mar suggested that it would be best for James to come at the head of 10,000 troops, although 5,000 might be enough. He also pointed out that George I could quite quickly have a large army at his disposal:

In a month's or six weeks' time the Government will have an army of well disciplined men, with all necessaries ... by a modest computation ... 32,000, besides the new troops that may be raised in England under the half pay officers.

But he deferentially added:

However, should the King (upon any secret intelligence he may have received or for other reasons which cannot be judged of here) continue resolved to risk everything and make the attempt without troops ...

and proceeded to give detailed suggestions of where and when James might best land if he came alone, although citing many drawbacks of this course of action. Some historians claim that James failed to make it clear to his supporters that he could not bring an army to Britain, and that they in turn failed to make it clear to him that the rising would not succeed without one. The fault lies not with the writers of the letters, who made their respective positions quite explicit, but with the readers, who saw only what they wanted.

Mar's letter seems to have taken James by surprise. His reply was delayed and lacking in enthusiasm:

> ... the reason why he [James] did not sooner answer ... was the hurry and incertainty he has been in in relation to his lawsuite [*the rebellion*], in which there has been so much darkness and so many rubs in the way that he can say at present nothing positive to it ... In the meantime 'tis a sensible comfort to me to see of one of Mr. Naper's [*Mar's*] experience and good sense so hearty in my cause, and so exact in the accounts he gives me of it.... I am glad you are going to see Mr. Sanders [*going to Scotland*].

Louis XIV had agreed to supply the Jacobites with arms that were loaded on to ships waiting at Le Havre: thousands of muskets and swords, barrels of powder, field guns and ammunition. But when Louis died on 1 September 1715 (N.S.) one of the Duke of Orléans' first acts as regent, prompted by the British minister Lord Stair, was to have the ships at Le Havre unloaded and the arms returned to the royal armouries.

On 20 September, Bolingbroke wrote an extremely pessimistic letter to Mar, pointing out that, among other difficulties,

> the whole coast from Jutland to Spain is against us; and unless the King steals off unknown, which to me appears almost impossible, considering the extent of country he must traverse, and the vigilance which is used in every part of France, he will either be seized or betrayed. The troops we hoped for from Sweden are refused us, and the bills which were given for their embarkation are returned. The money we expected from Spain is, in my opinion, still in the clouds, and was it actually in our hands we should be at a loss how to get it on board. Instead of having the arms which were promised us by the late King, it is become doubtful whether we shall have it in our power to carry off those which we have of our own.

In early October 1715, the Duke of Berwick broke some devastating news that he had earlier only hinted at: Orléans would not permit him to accompany James to Britain. Berwick was British by birth, the illegitimate son of James II and Arabella Churchill (Marlborough's sister), but James had given him permission to take French nationality. As a senior officer in the French army, he was not his own master. James was furious, believing that Berwick himself had made the decision not to go with him, and the relationship between the two men was permanently soured. But it was too late for second thoughts. By now the rising had begun and Mar's rebel army was already assembling in Perth. Bolingbroke was wrong about one thing, though: James did succeed in stealing off unknown (as described in CHAPTER 9).

Chapter 4

HINTS OF AN
ATTEMPT

PLANS FOR a large-scale uprising could not be kept secret. The purchase of arms and horses throughout Scotland in the winter of 1714/15 did not go unnoticed by the government, but it puzzled them because they could not believe that the Scots seriously intended to rebel. The rumours that circulated were largely fake news: the Duke of Berwick was coming; he would bring 10,000 men with him; huge shiploads of arms and money had already arrived in the north of Scotland.

Sir John Forester may have given much of his £4,000 to Highland chiefs, but Lowland gentry, such as the Master of Sinclair in Fife, were also buying arms and horses. Heritors considered themselves responsible for equipping their own men, and resented any interference, so preparations were often piecemeal and inadequate. Men of property would already own horses and guns but did not always realise that sporting guns and smart riding horses were not what they needed for military use.

On 9 August 1715, the Earl of Mar and Major-General George Hamilton left London. The story goes that King George had literally turned his back on Mar at a court reception on 1 August 1715 and this prompted him to set out on his incognito voyage to Scotland earlier than planned. In fact, he may have feared he was about to be arrested because his Jacobite activities had been discovered. Travelling under assumed names and accompanied by only three servants, Mar and Hamilton took with them £7,000 in cash donated by English Jacobites. At Gravesend in the Thames Estuary they embarked on a cargo boat, a collier on its way back north to Newcastle after carrying coal to London. This was an unglamorous, and probably uncomfortable, way to travel, but it served its purpose: they succeeded in leaving London unobserved and Mar's absence was not noticed for some days.

After changing ship at Newcastle, they arrived in Scotland on 16 August, landing on the Fife coast near Elie. Fife would have been familiar territory to Mar: his home estate was at Alloa, just a few miles further up the Firth of Forth. Mar and Hamilton first headed inland to the estate of James Bethune of Balfour, Hamilton's son-in-law, and the next day went on to Dupplin Castle, just six miles south-west of Perth. Dupplin was the estate of the Earl of Kinnoull, the father of Mar's first wife who had died in 1707. Kinnoull's younger son, John Hay, probably joined the party at this point.

From Dupplin, Mar's obvious route north would have taken him through the town of Perth itself, but this would have been far too public. Instead, they crossed the Tay some two miles below Perth, probably on Kinnoull's own land and safely out of sight of the town. They then stayed one night at Craighall, near Blairgowrie, an estate that was, until recently, owned for many generations by the Rattray family. Craighall is believed to be the estate on which Sir Walter Scott based 'Tully-Veolan', the picturesque home of the fictional Jacobite Bradwardine family in *Waverley*, his novel about the 1745 rising.

Mar's party of about eighteen men was then seen riding north through Strathardle towards Ashintully Castle near Kirkmichael, the home of the Spalding family. They then went on by the Spittal of Glenshee to Invercauld House, the home of John Farquharson. The Farquharsons of Invercauld were technically vassals of the Earls of Mar, although they had often been in conflict with them and in fact had burned down Braemar Castle in 1689, leaving the Earl of Mar without a home on his ancestral estate. Although Farquharson had no fondness for Mar, and left Invercauld rather than share the house with him, he remained loyal to the Jacobite cause. He fought under Mackintosh of Borlum at Preston and was taken prisoner after the battle. Pardoned and released from prison in August 1716, he returned to Scotland and played no further part in Jacobite politics.

From his base at Invercauld, Mar arranged a *tinchal*, a traditional Highland hunting party, as a pretext for calling together many of the local landowners and clan chiefs. The plan that Mar outlined to these men seems to have been that by starting a rebellion in Scotland the Jacobites would draw government forces away from England and encourage a popular rising there, thus attracting enough French support to overthrow the Whig regime.

At the same time, Mar wrote to his brother, Lord Grange, who was an eminent lawyer in Edinburgh, telling him that he had escaped from London because he was afraid of being arrested and now hoped that he would be allowed to live quietly on his Highland estate. Grange took no part in the Jacobite rising and it is not clear what his politics were, but he did as his brother asked and passed this misleading information on to the government. It may have helped to confuse them about Mar's motives, although not for long.

In late August, the news of Louis XIV's death reached Scotland. He had died on 21 August (O.S.), and according to an entry in Mrs Moncreiff the innkeeper's accounts (*see* p.46), the news had taken only four days to travel from Versailles to Perth:

	£	s	d
25/08/15 To the Mag[ist]rats with Cap bell of	06	8	10
Ed[inburgh] who brought the news of the			
French Kings death 6 bottles wine ale &c 14/10d			
The officers 6/-			

Either Captain Bell had had the fairest of fair winds in the North Sea or he was premature with his news. Louis had been on his deathbed for weeks and it is possible that rumours had been exaggerated.

Many Scottish Jacobites would not have given much thought to what Louis's death might mean for them; they did not think of the Jacobite cause in terms of its influence on European politics. Mar is reported to have responded that the Duke of Orléans would 'push the affair [the Jacobite rising] with more vigour than the old King'. As an experienced politician he ought to have had more insight, but perhaps he was making the best of the situation to encourage his supporters, as he would so often do in the months to come. General Hamilton was not so optimistic: when he heard the news of the French king's death, he is said to have suggested that he and Mar should escape to France to await a better opportunity.

On 6 September 1715, Mar raised the standard for King James VIII and III. According to local tradition, this ceremony took place on the site of the present Invercauld Arms Hotel, but so much legend has grown up around the event that it is impossible to know what really happened. Did hundreds of men witness it, or just a few dozen? Was the flag made of blue silk, embroidered by Lady Mar with mottos and coats of arms, or does that description relate to another flag raised at another time in another place? Did the gilded ball really fall off the top of the flagpole, or was that legend of ill omen created in retrospect after the failure of the rising? Even the contemporary accounts disagree.

The Presbyterian minister and historian Robert Wodrow, writing to the minister of the Scots congregation at Rotterdam in early September, summarised the few months leading up to the outbreak of the rising:

> When I saw you last, at the Assembly in May, we had some private hints of an attempt from France and the Pretender upon us, and they grew upon us in June and July, in the beginning of which our Jacobites, as is their way, began to set days for the arrival of the Pretender. Perhaps we were but too little alarmed with all, till upon the 20th of July, I think, the King came to the Parliament, and laid before them the certain accounts he had received of an attempt designed by the Pretender.

He is right about his dates. On 20 July 1715, the Duke of Montrose, who was then the Secretary of State responsible for Scotland, sent letters warning of an impending uprising to several local authorities in Scotland. At their meeting on 29 July 1715, the Dundee town council discussed news of 'a suddain invasion to be made by the Pretender with a forraigne force from parts beyond Sea' and agreed to guard the town. But although Dundee's town council was controlled by Whigs, the people of the town and the surrounding countryside were overwhelmingly Jacobite and it seems that the guard was never mounted.

The town council of Perth also took precautions, knowing that the town was likely to be attacked and occupied because of its strategic location. Both sides knew this: the Jacobite Master of Sinclair wrote, 'there was no other place where ane armie could been formed', and according to the anonymous Whig author of *News Letters of 1715–16*,

> certenly Perth will be a station they will affect to surprise as soon as any … it comands and can lay under contribution three or 4 shires the best in the Lowlands.

Perth commanded the routes from the west and south of Scotland towards the north and north-east. In addition, the burgh controlled the Bridge of Earn, a toll bridge four miles south of the town where the main routes to Stirling, Fife and Edinburgh crossed the River Earn, a tributary of the Tay.

Often described as the gateway to the Highlands, Perth was then regarded as being on the edge of civilised society. The River Tay was effectively a dividing line between the parts of Scotland that were largely under government control and those that were not. In 1715, the river was a real barrier; although it had been bridged at Perth in medieval times, the most recent bridge had been destroyed in the great flood of 1621. From then until 1776, when 'Smeaton's Bridge' (which is still in use) was opened, the Tay at Perth could be crossed only by boat. The town's traditional hinterland, the area in which the Perth Guildry had a trading monopoly, straddled this unofficial political and cultural boundary between Highlands and Lowlands.

The Scottish Highlands was regarded, even by people who lived only a day's journey away, as a wild and uncivilised region, inhabited by savages who spoke an incomprehensible language. The Highlanders were despised but feared, as a 1715 article in a London newspaper indicates:

> The meanest Man among them … is not without his Gun, his broad Sword, his Durk and his Target … The Men of the Meaner Sort are strong, large, made hardy, and very rugged; they are desperate, furious, and bloody Fellows … and are like so many Wild-Men.

They were also widely believed to be Catholics, although this is an oversimplification. Some clans were Catholic, but in the more remote areas organised religion suffered from a shortage of Gaelic-speaking

FIGURE 2. List of men appointed by the magistrates
to guard the ports in the daytime, 7 September 1715.
[Reproduced by permission of Perth & Kinross Archives, B59/30/2.]

clergy of any denomination to serve the large and inaccessible parishes. Presbyterian missionary work went on throughout the eighteenth century but was not far advanced in 1715.

Perth's position on the boundary was reflected in its divided political and religious loyalties: in central Scotland, Presbyterian Whigs were in the majority, but the north-east was regarded as an Episcopalian and Jacobite stronghold. The religious conflict affected everyone, not just men who were ready to take up arms. For Presbyterians, the situation was clear: James, whom they called the Pretender, was a Papist and if he became king they would be subjected to absolutist Catholic rule, forced conversions, and nameless tyrannies. He must be stopped. For the Episcopalian Jacobites, it was much more nuanced. James and his advisers knew his path to the throne would be much easier if he renounced his Catholic faith, but he would not do it. This was one of the few points on which he could not be talked round by any of his favourites. But his supporters in Scotland believed in the principle of a hereditary monarchy, and their loyalty to the Stuarts was only strengthened by the harassment their religion had suffered since the Revolution. They were prepared to accept James's personal Catholicism but expected him to restore Episcopalianism in Scotland and support the established church in England. Propaganda in the form of sermons and pamphlets, such as those printed in Perth by Robert Freebairn during the Jacobite occupation, stressed James's Scottish ancestry and his aim to dissolve the Union with England, reassuring readers that their fears of 'popery' were imaginary and that James was no more foreign than the Lutheran, German-speaking, George I.

In the 1680s, during the reign of James II, Perth's town council had been Episcopalian and had actively harassed local Presbyterians (*see* CHAPTER 2): since the Revolution the Presbyterian Whigs had been in charge. Both parties bore grudges and had long memories, and relations between Whig and Jacobite burgesses in Perth were not cordial. In 1715, the Jacobite burgesses ('Torie burghers' as Sinclair calls them) were still numerous enough, and influential enough, to ensure the bloodless surrender of the town and to administer it during the months of military occupation.

In the summer of 1715, Perth took more effective precautions than Dundee had been able to do. Men were enlisted to guard the ports (gates) of the town (*see* FIGURE 2), attempts were made to repair the ruined medieval walls and repair the gates, houses were searched for weapons, and ammunition was prepared. For 27 July 1715, the accounts of John Strachan, the burgh treasurer, list three items of expenditure (in pounds Scots):

	£	s	d
To the boatmen waiting 5 nights at this side att 6/- a night & ale	01	12	00
For paper to make cartrages and to the officers	00	16	00
Spent by the Magistrats and given to the men that searcht for arms	03	06	06

Keeping the boats on the west (town) side of the river overnight, so that no one could cross under cover of darkness, was an obvious security measure.

Cartridges for the flintlock muskets and pistols then in use had to be made by hand, by wrapping a lead ball and a measured amount of black powder in a cylinder of strong paper. 'Making cartrages' appears several times in Strachan's accounts, and altogether he spent £105 15s. on 'powder, ball, and lead' for the town between 25 July and 15 September 1715. Despite this, a shortage of powder was one of the Master of Sinclair's many complaints when he first arrived in Perth: 'the few pounds of pouder they pickt up in the toun, which I don't believe were above five or six'. Sinclair, who had military experience, thought little of the town's preparations.

A list of expenses submitted to the town council by Janet Moncreiff also yields interesting information about what was going on in Perth that summer. Mrs Moncreiff was the proprietor of an inn that was evidently much patronised by the magistrates (the bailies) and other councillors, at the burgh's expense. The inn's till also seems to have been used as a source of ready cash for small expenditures, which Mrs Moncreiff would later claim back from the burgh treasurer. Her accounts confirm the preparations being made in late July:

	£	s	d
27/07 At night w[i]th the Baylies & officers			
of the Guard 19/-	01	11	0
Of[ficer]s 12/-			
28/07 Being the day th[e] Inhabitants were			
drawn out under arms 13 bottle wine			
10 bottles ale, bread 6/- £12:15:0			
28/07 To be a part of the guard who searched			
the town for arms 14/-			
officers 12/- £01:06:0	14	01	0

The 'officers of the Guard' who drank with the bailies were military men or militia; those who received twelve shillings were the town's officers, civilians whose duties included acting as bodyguards to the provost and bailies. There normally seem to have been four of these men in attendance and 'Officers 12/-' appears frequently in Mrs Moncreiff's expenses.

The town council took the further precaution of asking the Duke of Atholl to send men to help defend the town. Atholl was the most important local nobleman, legally a feudal overlord with powers of life and death in his regality, which covered much of the county. He also embodied the more modern power of King George: he had been the sheriff of Perthshire since 1695 and was appointed lord lieutenant of the county in August 1715. As lord lieutenant he was the monarch's personal representative and controlled the militia, and as sheriff he was responsible for royal justice. Nevertheless, his political allegiance was questionable. He had strongly opposed the Union, but subsequently became one of the Scottish representative peers in the London parliament. Until he came down strongly on the government side in 1715, the Jacobites had believed that Atholl would lead the rising. Despite the duke's decision, the Murray family's loyalties were divided, and three of Atholl's sons, including his heir, joined the rising. Whichever side won, the Atholl estate would remain in the family.

Atholl's men had arrived in Perth by 15 September and their officers were entertained by the magistrates, as Mrs Moncreiff's accounts for that day show:

		£	s	d
15/09	Spent by the Mag[ist]rats with the			
	Officers of the Duke of Atholls men	03	08	o
	11 pints & 18 bottles ale			
	1 Mutchken Brandy 2 duz: rolls			
	To the Town Officers		06	o
	Spent that day by Baylie Ferguson & o[the]rs		13	o
	At night spent by the Magistrats	01	04	o
	To the officers and o[ther]s a leg of			
	mutton & ale	00	16	o

The next day, 16 September, the town would come under attack. The events of that day would show that the loyalties of the men Atholl had sent to defend the town were as conflicted as those of the Murray family themselves.

Chapter 5
THE STORIE OF
PEARTH BEING TAKNE

IN OUTLINE, the account of how the Jacobites took Perth in September 1715 is common to all the historical sources. The (Whig) Duke of Atholl sent a contingent of men to help guard the town. The (Whig) town council and burgesses armed themselves as best they could. Colonel John Hay and a troop of Jacobite horsemen were lurking on the far side of the river Tay. Local Jacobites commandeered boats and ferried Hay and his men across the river into the town. Many of Atholl's men decided to join them, the Whigs realised that they were outnumbered, and the town fell into Jacobite hands without bloodshed.

As with so much of the story of 1715, the contemporary sources disagree about many details of what the Master of Sinclair calls 'the storie of Pearth being takne', such as the numbers of men involved and even the date of the event. Some historians give this as the 14th, some as the 18th, but the Guild Book of Perth's Guildry Incorporation and the minutes of St John's kirk session both state that the rising in Perth began on 16 September. These independent records, written in the town itself very soon after the event, are unlikely to be wrong.

Did Hay have forty horsemen, 100, or 200? Could Provost Austin possibly have assembled as many as 300 or 400 armed burgesses, or more likely thirty or forty? Sinclair provides a plausible reason for such discrepancies and exaggerations:

> those in a countrie like ours, who were not used to war, and conse-
> quentlie to see any number of men together, with the terrour that
> was upon them, imagined everie hundred men to be a thousand.

The large numbers that appeared in the earliest newspaper reports would have been reported by men who had left Perth in a hurry to escape the Jacobite takeover. These men would not have wanted to give the impression that they had been ousted by puny forces, and, according to Sinclair, they reported to the government that 'there were some thousand Highlandmen got into Pearth'.

The number of men the Duke of Atholl sent to Perth is also variously reported, estimates ranging from 150 to 400. The treasurer's accounts (likely to be an accurate source) mention rations for 110 men. Despite being quite lavishly entertained by the magistrates at Mrs Moncreiff's inn on 15 September (*see* p.48), around half of Atholl's men chose to help the Jacobites when they arrived. Although they had obeyed the duke's order to go to Perth, these men were evidently not prepared to take up arms against Colonel Hay and his Jacobite horsemen, being (according to Sinclair) 'naturallie well inclined to the [Jacobite] cause', as were three of the duke's sons.

Two local men who played an important part in the Jacobite takeover of the town were James Ramsay and James Freebairn. Freebairn, the younger brother of Robert Freebairn who was soon to set up the Jacobite printing press in the town, was an excise officer based in Perth. Excise officers were unpopular, especially since the imposition of the malt tax in Scotland in 1713, but the job would have provided opportunities for meeting with local merchants, many of whom were Jacobite sympathisers (the 'Torie burghers'). James Ramsay was the Earl of Kinnoull's factor. When he was taken prisoner in early 1716, he was described as having 'headed the inhabitants at surprising the town'. An estate factor was an important man: he managed the day-to-day affairs of an estate and dealt with the tenants on behalf of the landowner. Lord Kinnoull owned much property around Perth, including Dupplin to the south and Balhousie less than half a mile north of the city walls. Ramsay would have been a familiar figure to estate tenants and would routinely have visited them in the course of his work. Both he and Freebairn would have been able to move around the area and meet people without attracting suspicion.

Ramsay's Kinnoull connection is significant. Colonel Hay was the Earl of Kinnoull's younger son. He had set out from Dupplin with the

Earl of Mar but was not present at the raising of the standard in Braemar. He had stayed behind at Lord Nairne's house just north of Perth, with orders from Mar to secure the town for the Jacobites. Hay's rank gives the impression that he was an experienced military officer, but in fact he was only twenty-four years of age in 1715 and had bought his colonelcy in the Guards just the year before. Sinclair, sarcastic as usual, describes him as 'a young lad ... latelie come from schoole, and ... all the service he had done was to have mounted the guard once or twice at St James's'. Although at this time Lord Kinnoull himself was briefly imprisoned in Edinburgh Castle, and his heir Lord Dupplin was in the Tower of London, the earl's younger son with the earl's factor backing him up could bring powerful pressure to bear on estate tenants.

The Master of Sinclair was not an impartial witness, and much of what he says in his *Memoirs of the Insurrection in Scotland in 1715* is coloured by his deep hatred of the Earl of Mar, but he generally seems to be a reliable source on practical matters and provides the most detailed account of the period immediately before and after the taking of Perth. According to Sinclair, by mid-September many Jacobites from Fife had gone north to Perthshire, but were essentially leaderless, not in contact with Mar and at a loss what to do next. Despite his limited military experience, John Hay was able to gather them together and, with local help, ferry them over the Tay into Perth. As a Fife man himself, Sinclair would have known many of the men concerned and would be unlikely to get the number far wrong, so his estimate of forty is probably more reliable than the 100 or 200 mentioned in newspaper reports.

On the day, the decision of the Atholl men to support the Jacobites swung the balance in favour of the attackers. Another decisive factor was Provost Austin calling for 'no blood, no blood'. The two sides agreed a truce: the Jacobites took over the town without a fight, and men who wanted to leave the town were free to go.

The formal proclamation of James VIII as king was an important feature of the Jacobite takeover, and seems to have followed a similar ritual in all the Scottish burghs they occupied. In any town, the mercat (market) cross was the place where important public announcements were made. Perth's medieval mercat cross had been destroyed by Cromwell's troops in 1651. Its replacement, a stone monument with steps surmounted by a cross, was built in 1669 on the same spot in the centre of the High Street, near the Skinnergate (sadly, it was demolished in 1765 because it got in the way of traffic). It was decorated for the occasion, and the proclamation ceremony was accompanied by the ringing of the church bells and the drinking of loyal toasts such as 'No Union!' and (ironically enough) 'No popery!'.

In its report of the taking of Perth, the *St. James's Evening Post* also mentions the proclamation of James as king in other northern burghs: Montrose, Brechin, Aberbrothick (Arbroath), and Inverness. The report states that in all these towns except Perth the burgh councils were generally Jacobite sympathisers. On 20 September, the Earl Marischal proclaimed James VIII at the mercat cross of Aberdeen, apparently unopposed. The largest town in the north-east of Scotland, Aberdeen had a strong Episcopalian tradition: Presbyterianism and its accompanying Whig politics had been slow to take hold. When the Jacobites first arrived there, the town council was nominally Whig, but by the end of September a Jacobite council had quietly taken its place. There may even have been collusion between the Whig and Jacobite urban elites to ensure that the town remained in safe hands whatever the outcome of the rebellion.

In Dundee, Jacobites from the local area threatened the town in early September and finally took it over on 16 September, the same day as Hay entered Perth. The Whig town council had pleaded for government help, and when it did not come, they fled. Dundee was held by the Jacobites throughout the rising, but there are no extant records of town council meetings after 31 July until a new Whig council was elected in April 1716.

All the burghs in this north-east corner of Scotland seem to have been in Jacobite hands before the end of September, with little or no actual violence. In Perth there does not seem to have been any collusion between Whig and Jacobite burgesses, although Provost Austin's order to avoid bloodshed may well have been prompted by a desire to minimise damage to the town and its people.

As well as asking the Duke of Atholl to send men, Austin had requested help from another local magnate, the Earl of Rothes, who was the sheriff and lord lieutenant of the neighbouring county of Fife. Rothes, a loyal Whig, who had been supplied with arms by the government, attempted to form the men of the county into an armed force, the *posse comitatus*. The heritors who would have been the natural leaders of such a force were largely Jacobites, and most of them ignored the order. Humbler men urged on by their (Presbyterian, Whig) parish ministers, assembled at Cash Moor near Strathmiglo on 18 September, but they evidently had no desire to fight; when they heard that the Jacobites had already taken Perth, they fled.

Austin and several members of the town council had immediately left Perth under the terms of the truce. According to Sinclair, 'some of them road post to Edinbourgh to inform the Gouvernment'. Some headed instead for Stirling, where Argyll's government troops were based. Prominent Whigs who remained, 'James Austen, merchant there, his son [the provost's brother and nephew], John Lindsay, merchant, and John Nimmo, maltman, Archibald Brough, writer, James McMichael, Robert Melville, and David Taylor, merchant, Henry Brown, glover, and Patrick Smith, flesher' were imprisoned in the Perth tolbooth but soon released on condition they behaved themselves 'peacably and discreetly'.

The first report of how the Jacobite rebels had taken Perth and imprisoned some of the Whig burgesses appeared in London newspapers within a week. Slightly later accounts gave more detail, naming 'Coll. Hay, Son to the Earl of Kinnoul, Coll. [John] Balfour, and Major [Henry] Balfour, with some others, particularly Freebairn, a present Collector of the Excise' as among the men responsible.

Once they had proclaimed the town's allegiance to King James, the Jacobites began to take practical measures to secure the town, gathering up all the arms and public money they could find. James Freebairn, whom Mar appointed as his deputy treasurer, handed over the money he had in hand from the collection of excise dues. He later reported:

> at the time the town of Perth was reduced to his Majesty's obedience I had 170l. [£170] sterling [£2,040 Scots] of the public money in my hands which I applied for the payment of the army, which subsisted it for four days ...

A temporary local government was installed. A commission from Mar dated 21 September stated that this was necessary because 'The Provost and Baillies of the said burgh of Perth have refused and declined to act in their office of Magistracie and partly deserted the town'. Hay was appointed as governor of the town and five 'commissioners' were named:

> Patrick Davidson late provost of Perth, Patrick Hay, Lawfull son to the deceasd Patrick Hay late provost there, Mr James Smyth Chirurgeon Apothecary in Perth and Nathaniel Fyfe and Mark Wood Merchants there.

The commissioners were appointed to serve 'until Magistrats and other officers be duly and Regularly chosen and authorised therein'. By coincidence, late September (Michaelmas) was the usual time of year for the election of burgh officers. The commissioners met on 23 September and elections took place on 1 October (*see* CHAPTER 6).

Although the original attacking force had been small, Perth was soon to be the military headquarters for a considerable army. The first reinforcements to arrive were 200 men from Angus, under Lord Strathmore. Poorly trained and equipped, they would not have been able to defend the town against the Duke of Argyll, who had around 1,500 men at Stirling, only forty miles away. But the early reports greatly magnified the number of rebels in Perth, and Argyll remained in camp, protected by the guns of Stirling Castle, rather than risking his men.

The Master of Sinclair arrived, with fifty more horsemen from Fife, shortly after Strathmore and his men. At that time the Jacobite strength in Perth amounted to

> a hundred horse, with what I brought alonge with me, and tuo hundred Low Countrie men, who, I knew, were not at all used to armes, and fiftie Highlandmen, of those who came first into Pearth by the Duke of Athole's order.

Sinclair was evidently determined to find fault, and he describes at some length how poorly prepared and equipped the Jacobites were. Strathmore's 'Low Countrie' men had 'old rustie musketts, who had never fired one in their lives, and without pouder and flints' and the fifty Highlandmen were no better equipped. Sinclair immediately made himself unpopular with Colonel Hay and the Jacobite commissioners by criticising their efforts to improve the town's defences, which he believed were quite inadequate. He told them that the town walls and gates – which they had been at some pains to refurbish – should be reduced in height so that the defenders could fire over them. The south side of the town had no wall, being protected by what Sinclair called 'a ditch full of water, seven foot deep, for three foot in the middle onlie, and not ten foot over'. This was a stretch of the lade, an artificial waterway drawing water from the River Almond to power the town's mills. For centuries the lade had formed part of the town's defences, serving as a moat. The lade still exists, part of it running under the town's streets, but in 1715 it must have been a more imposing body of water than the shallow stream that can be seen today north of the old city mills. Sinclair recommended that a wooden palisade should be built behind the lade and it seems that this was done, although his suggestions about lowering the walls and gates were not accepted.

Meanwhile the Earl of Mar was travelling south to Perth, via Moulin, Logierait, and Dunkeld, collecting men and proclaiming King James on his way. Recruitment was hindered by the unusual lateness of the harvest that year. Men whose livelihood depended on their crops were understandably reluctant to be dragged away from the fields at such a time, especially as the harvest was plentiful, but early eighteenth-century Scotland was a hierarchical society where men were expected to obey their social superiors; so, however unwillingly, they went.

By 28 September, Mar had reached Perth, bringing with him around 2,500 foot and 500 horse, and was soon joined by many more. From the end of September 1715 until the end of January 1716, many thousands of men and horses had to be accommodated. The total number is unknown: the sources give round numbers that vary widely and are often implausibly high. Some authors suggest there were as many as 16,000, but a maximum of 9,000 seems more likely. Some of the men were eventually billeted on householders, but there simply were not enough houses in the town to accommodate them all. The hearth tax records of the 1690s list only

FIGURE 3. Huntingtower Castle, just outside Perth beside the road to Crieff. The fifteenth- and sixteenth-century defensible towers are linked by a more domestic seventeenth-century range.
[Photograph © Roben Antoniewicz.]

984 taxable households in Perth and its suburbs, and that number might even have decreased by 1715.

In fact, it is clear from letters and other documents that many of the Jacobite soldiers were not quartered in Perth itself. The first men to arrive had camped on the North Inch (a large area of common land adjacent to the town, now parkland but then used for grazing). Officers and gentlemen who could afford it found private lodgings or inn rooms in the town. Later arrivals found accommodation 'in Barns &c.' on the farmland that immediately surrounded the town, such as the Glover Incorporation's property at Tullylumb (*see* p.67). Many of them were quartered much further from the town. As early as 8 October, the Marquis of Huntly wrote to John Gordon of Glenbucket, 'I hope there will be room for the rest of the foot when they come up at Cupar' (he meant Coupar Angus, which is twelve miles north of Perth). Other contingents were based in the Carse of Gowrie, east of the town, and Strathearn, to the west. The latter were almost within reach of attack by some of Argyll's men who were based at Castle Campbell, just on the other side of the Ochil Hills. Men based in these outlying areas were a long way from any military discipline that might prevail in Perth itself, and they were not slow to take advantage of this (*see* CHAPTER 7).

The Earl of Mar dated some of his letters from Huntingtower Castle (*see* FIGURE 3), then a country home just to the west of Perth that belonged to the Duke of Atholl. Later, he and his senior officers set up their headquarters at Scone Palace, some two miles outside Perth on the other side of the Tay. The Scone estate belonged to Lord Stormont, a Jacobite peer whose daughter Marjorie was the wife of Colonel Hay, but the house was not then used by the family and seems to have been partly derelict, or at least unfurnished. (In the early nineteenth century it was enlarged and rebuilt into the handsome Georgian house we can see today.)

Although Mar was accumulating a large number of men, he was very short of experienced officers. At one time there had been hopes of bringing over hundreds of Irish officers from recently disbanded regiments of the French army, but although often discussed in Jacobite correspondence this was never a practical possibility. Mar himself had no military experience. General Hamilton, who had travelled with him from London, had spent his military career in the Dutch forces and was accustomed to leading trained and disciplined soldiers, very different from the irregulars who followed the Jacobite banner in 1715. Hamilton had served briefly as a Tory member of parliament and seems to have agreed with Mar's political opinions, which may explain his involvement in the 1715 rising. Mar must have thought that the presence of such a senior military officer would aid an armed rebellion, but it did not work out well. James Keith, the brother of the Earl Marischal, reflected years later that

> Hamilton, who tho' an old officer, was not in the least equal to the affair he was to undertake, for tho' he had served long and with very good reputation in the Dutch troops, yet being a man whom only experience, not natural genious, had made an officer, he did not know how to make use of his new troops, who are of a disposition as hot and quick as the Dutch are slow and flegmatick ...

In Perth, Hamilton seems to have been quickly sidelined by Mar. Sinclair comments:

> In the beginning Generall Hamilton gave out the orders, and seemed to doe all things that belonged to the militarie; but, by degrees, that pouer was takne from him, and my Lord Mar took upon him the management of most things himself.

Throughout the Jacobite campaign, the lack of military discipline was a problem. Neither Hamilton nor Mar was able to impose an adequate command structure: social status always seemed to trump military rank or ability. Each heritor, however inexperienced, considered himself responsible for his own men, and resented anyone else taking command of them or even providing them with equipment. Mar bought their compliance by conferring inflated military ranks:

> picking out all the sprightlieft younge gentlemen to make officers amongst the foot, which there was no dissuadeing them from doeing, because they got the rank of Captains, Liutenants, and Ensignes.

There were few experienced officers other than Sinclair himself, who had been lucky to escape execution after being court-martialled for killing two fellow officers. Colonel Urquhart (Sinclair spells it Urchard) had served in an infantry regiment until 1714, and the two Balfours (who were remote cousins, not brothers as Sinclair says) had served several decades earlier. Mar relied heavily on William Clephane, a major in the government army who had defected to the Jacobites. Despite his relatively junior rank, Clephane took on much of the intensive training that was required to form the Jacobites in Perth into a military unit, but his attempts to form regiments and drill the troops in the conventional way were often ignored. Mar, ever the politician, often preferred not to disoblige men of his own rank by insisting they should do as they were told.

Supplying the growing army with food, weapons, and equipment was a major concern. The logistical framework required to organise accommodation, food, and pay for an army simply did not exist in Perth in 1715. Mar, who seems to have been a micro-manager by nature and had years of experience behind a desk rather than leading an army, took on much of this responsibility himself. In the early weeks of the occupation he wrote many requisitioning orders. He ordered the magistrates of burghs such as Montrose and Aberdeen to send him recruits and whatever they had of military supplies, such as lead and gunpowder. The Jacobites were chronically short of firearms: the thousands of muskets and other weapons they had expected to be sent from France would never arrive. Many of the arms the rebels brought in with them were unsuitable, old, or defective. Instead, Mar ordered Lochaber axes, 150 from Montrose and 300 from Aberdeen. A Lochaber axe (*see* FIGURE 4) would have been relatively cheap and easy for a local blacksmith to make, although men would need some training to be able to use it effectively against cavalry in battle.

It was not only weapons that were required; many of the Highlanders evidently arrived barefoot, and there seems to have been an insatiable demand for shoes:

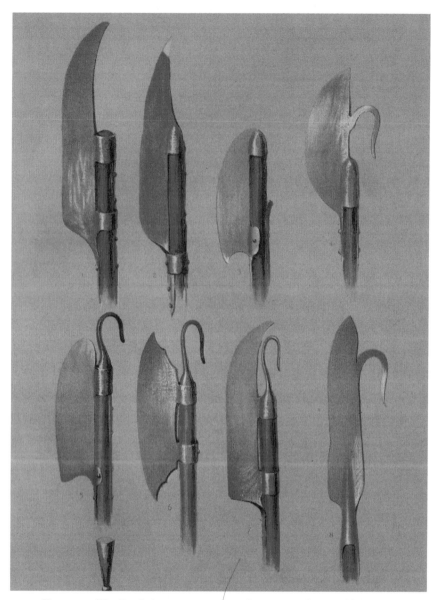

FIGURE 4. The Lochaber axe was a simple weapon that could be very effective against cavalry. The large blade about 18 inches (45 cm) long was mounted on a wooden shaft about five feet (1.8 m) long.
[From *Ancient Scottish Weapons* by James Drummond, George Waterson, 1881]

These [orders] are to impower you to search at Auchterarder, Denin [Dunning], Tullibardin, Muthil and Creiff for all the Leather and made Shoes which are fit for the Use of the Army, and to seize the said Leather and Shoes ... and you are to direct the Proprietors of the said Leather and Shoes to come here and receive the Money due to them ... The Account of Leather is to be sent to Colonel Balfour, Governour of Perth, and the Proprietors directed to wait upon him for their Payment.

Within a few weeks, payments were in the form of scribbled receipts. The recipients of these chits would not only be deprived of their goods or produce but would also have to travel miles to Perth to receive payment – and perhaps not very adequate payment – for what had been seized.

On 19 October, Mar appointed a commissary of the stores, whose orders were

to receive, and grant Receipts for what Quantities of Meal and Breads shall be brought into you from Time to Time for the Use of the Army, and to give out, and distribute the same as you shall be directed

Even after appointing a commissary, Mar still signed many requisitions himself. As well as orders for bread and copious amounts of wine, on 21 October he wrote:

You are hereby impowered and required forthwith to seize the Ship or Barge that came loaded with Onions from Holland, now lying in the Harbour of Montrose ...

By late October, a Committee of Provisions was in operation. Andrew Morison of Dundee wrote to the committee on 28 October:

I have in all haste shipped on Board John Bruce's Boat Eighteen hundred twenty and four brown Loaves, exactly of the former Sizes, and would have sent twenty five Bolls of Lundie's Oat-Meal which came only to me this Afternoon, but your Orders coming so late, the Boat could not receive it and the Bread both, being now eleven a-Clock at Night, I presume to put you in Mind of the Country-mens Secks [sacks], if possible to return them.

It would have been quicker and easier to transport bulky goods from Dundee to Perth by river than by road, especially on an incoming tide, and this was probably the usual route until the river froze.

Mar has often been criticised for his decision to keep his troops in Perth for so long rather than confronting Argyll early on, when he had a considerable numerical advantage. It is an arguable point, but it is worth remembering that his recruits were largely inexperienced men without even basic training, not a ready-made army. On 12 October, 2,000 men were dispatched under William Mackintosh of Borlum on an expedition to Edinburgh and beyond (*see* CHAPTER 8). It seems likely that Borlum would have been allocated the best troops available for this ambitious venture, leaving the less experienced men to undergo further training in and around Perth. There was also a considerable turnover in the Jacobite forces as the desertion rate was high: men who had joined the colours unwillingly took advantage of any opportunity to go home. On the whole, the Jacobite officers seem to have done a creditable job in creating an army of perhaps 8,000 men to march out to Sheriffmuir only eight weeks after the first of them arrived in Perth.

Chapter 6

THEIR PRESENT
PRESSING BUSINESS

T HE ELECTION of town councillors in Perth in September
1715 followed the traditional procedure, with names being chosen
by the burgesses from leets (lists) provided by the merchant guild
and the trades. The only difference this time was that only names
acceptable to the Jacobite commissioners were on the lists. With many of
the Whig burgesses having left the town or being locked up in the
tolbooth, there would have been a majority of Jacobite burgesses who
were eligible to participate in council elections and serve as councillors.
Patrick Hay was elected provost, sheriff, and coroner (at this time it was
normal for these three positions to be combined, the duties of the sheriff
being carried out by a deputy). Four bailies acted as the burgh's magistrates:
Nathaniel Fyffe, James Smyth, and John Young were the merchant
bailies, and James Swells, a barber and wigmaker, was the trades bailie.
Mark Wood was the dean of guild, the Guildry's representative on the
town council. John Gourlay, a maltman (and also a writer, or solicitor),
was the burgh treasurer. Other merchant councillors were John Paterson,
John Murray, George Threipland, Andrew Walker, John Strachan, George
Wilson, and George Moncreiff. Joseph Taylor for the hammermen (metal-
workers), John Bayne for the wrights (woodworkers and stonemasons),
and Charles Alison for the fleshers (butchers) were trades councillors.
Several of these names appear in the investigations into Episcopalian
worship discussed in CHAPTER 2: Mark Wood, Nathaniel Fyffe, Joseph
Taylor, George Threipland, George Wilson, and John Gourlay.

The new council met for the first time on 3 October. One of its first
actions was to decree that the town should recruit two companies for the

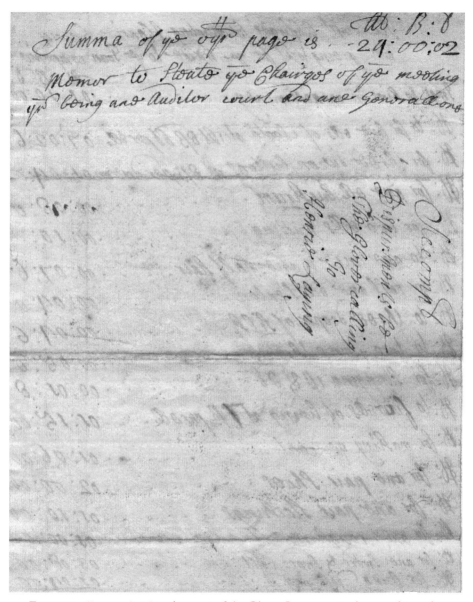

FIGURE 5. *Above and right* – Account of the Glover Incorporation's expenditure for
Henry Laing *'on going out for the trade to the town companies'*.
[Reproduced by permission of Perth & Kinross Archives MS67/17/Bundle 177.]

Accompt Chairges for munting Henrie Laing
when going out for ye traide to ye Toun companie

	lb	s	d
Imp: to him in earnest money	05	10	00
It: to for five ells of cloath at ... 8/3 6d per ell	07	02	6
It: for three dizen buttons at 8/3 per dizen	01	04	0
It: for ane ell buckrum	00	08	0
It: for two ells wadding	00	10	
It: to ane unce & ane half hair	00	07	6
It: to half ane ell Stenton	00	04	0
It: to three drope of silk	00	04	6
It: to two unces threed	00	05	0
It: for stringing 1/3 & 3d	00	05	8
It: to five ells of lining at 7/3 per ell	05	15	00
It: for making ye coat	01	06	00
It: for ane pair shoes	02	00	00
It: for ane pair stockings	05	10	00
It: for ane rough wallat	05	00	00
It: for ane sword & sword bell	03	08	00
It: for foure days pay	05	04	00

Jacobite cause, each of forty men plus officers. Several paragraphs in the minutes of this meeting record a discussion of how important it was that the Perth companies should have precedence in the line of march.

The dean of guild relayed the council's decision to the Guildry. As an inducement, men who served in one of the town's companies for three months would be given their burgess ticket without having to pay the usual entry fee, which for a 'stranger', i.e. a man whose father or father-in-law was not a guildsman, was the considerable sum of 100 merks (£66 6s. 8d. Scots).

The order was proclaimed around the town several times by the town's officers with a piper and drummer (the glovers paid £1 Scots towards this publicity), but the response was not enthusiastic. It was taking too long to attract volunteers and in the end some men had to be conscripted. At their meeting on 19 October, the Guildry discussed the problem:

> ... the two companies not being as yet compleat, and the time running on It was Resolved and agreed to by the Town Council for the more speedy and effectual Levying and compleating the Said companies without loss of time that there should be Sixteen men levied by way of Militia th[ere]of eight from the Guildry and eight from the trades... They ... agreed that there be money levied out from the particular persons of the Guildry to be given to those who will ingage voluntarily .... the Sum of twenty Shillings Sterling be payed to those who will ingage for the Gildry and this beside their freedom of burgeship and that the sum of fourty shillings be given to those who are already burgesses.

Eventually enough men were enlisted. Six of these Jacobite recruits – Alexander Gibson, Adam Grinsell, two men called Robert Miller, Duncan Our (Ure), and George Philp – were among the men who had been paid 6d. or 8d. a day to guard the ports in September (*see* FIGURE 2). Evidently, they were signing up for money, not for ideological reasons.

The council's original plan had been that the provost would head one of the town's companies; and the dean of guild, the other, but by the next council meeting they had been firmly told it was better for these officials to stay in Perth and attend to the town's business. Mr John Paterson (unlike other burgesses he is always referred to deferentially as *Mr* Paterson) became the captain of one company, and Joseph Taylor of the other.

One of the men who enlisted was Henry Laing, a member of the Glover Incorporation. Leather goods (including gloves) were one of Perth's most important exports, and the glovers had been one of the main trades in the town for centuries. This is probably why Sir Walter Scott, in his novel *The Fair Maid of Perth*, chose to make his heroine the daughter of a prosperous glover. The glover calling, as it was informally known, had become wealthy and owned property in and around the town, including farmland at Tullylumb that had belonged to the Carmelite order (the White Friars) before the Reformation. The glovers spent £29 0s. 2d. on recruiting and equipping Henry Laing (*see* FIGURE 5). By far the most expensive item was his coat, which cost altogether £13 8s. 2d. Made from five ells of cloth, with thirty-six buttons, embroidery, and braid, it must have been a magnificent garment. A Scottish ell was just over a yard (94 cm). Buckram, [horse]hair, wadding, and stenten (stenting) would have been used for stiffening and padding parts of the garment. Stringing could be any kind of braid or piping. A drap (drop) of silk is a sixteenth of an ounce, less than 2 grams, perhaps embroidery thread. The 'rough wallet' is presumably some kind of leather knapsack. It is interesting that the sword, perhaps not a high-quality weapon, cost so much less than the coat.

Although the Jacobite town council was essentially a puppet regime that took orders from the Earl of Mar and his assistants, for a short time it acted as any council was expected to do. Its election followed the traditional procedure, it set prices for commodities (known as the fiars prices), and the bailies presided over the burgh court. James Smyth, the former army surgeon who was one of the bailies, also seems to have acted as a kind of liaison officer between the council and the military authorities. The Master of Sinclair writes sarcastically that Colonel Hay had made Smyth 'Major de la Place' (a title given to a high-ranking officer in charge of a garrison's administration).

After he arrived in Perth, one of Mar's first requirements was money. He had brought £7,000 sterling with him from London but had already spent much of this on recruiting men further north. Mar ordered the town council of Perth to collect land cess (land tax) for him:

Our Sovereign Lord James the Eight having been pleased to Intrust Me with the direction of his affairs, and the command of his forces in Scotland, And it being absolutely necessary to raise money for their Support and Mantainance, These are Therefore in his Name, Requiring and Commanding You the Lord Provost Baillies and town Council of the Burgh of Perth to raise & levy six Months Cess, extending to the sum of One hundred and fifty pounds four shill and nine pence Starling money [more than £1,800 Scots], to be ... the Usuall Manner and payed in to James Freebairn collector Appointed for yt and on Thursday next the sixth day of October Instant betwixt the hours of ten and twelve in the forenoon With Certification that if you faill theirin, you will be quartered upon and poynded, And ordain these presents to be published at the Mercate Cross of Perth that none may pretend ignorance Given at the Camp of Perth the fourth day of October One thousand seven hundered and fifetein years.

The order is dated 4 October, and Mar demands that the money be paid just two days later. Anyone who disobeys will be punished, and these punishments are not trivial. Being quartered upon means that soldiers will be billeted in your house, able to use your goods freely; being poynded means that your goods will be impounded and sold to raise the money due.

Mar sent similar proclamations to burgh councils and country land-owners throughout the area his men occupied. He demanded cess at double rates from landowners who were not favourable to the Jacobite cause. A counter-proclamation by Argyll forbade these cess payments, but Mar's men were on the spot to enforce the tax collection, and Argyll's were not. No records exist of the total amount raised, but it would have been considerable. James Oliphant of Gask, a loyal Jacobite, paid £95 8s. for his property at Williamston and £210 for his main estate at Gask, and there were many such estates in the area.

As stated earlier, one of the duties of the town's bailies was to act as magistrates. There are records of sentences passed in the burgh court by Nathaniel Fyffe, James Smyth, and James Swells between October 1715 and January 1716. The recorded cases all relate in some way to the occupation of the town. On 12 October, Margaret Hall appeared before bailies Fyffe, Smyth, and Swells accused of pickpocketing. She was ordered to be whipped through the town, but in view of her 'Ingenuitie' (i.e. ingenuousness – she may have been young and/or foolish) the sentence was mitigated to banishment 'never to return'. On the same day, John Scot 'taylor and postmaster' complained that James Matthew (a maltman) had abused him when he was pressing horses for the service of the army, calling him bugger and 'other opprobrious words and expressions' and threatening to beat him, because he thought these demands were excessive. Matthew was fined £10 Scots.

On 29 November 1715 bailies Fyffe, Smyth, and Swells dealt with a more complicated case. Elizabeth Hammilton was accused of stealing 'cloaths' including an apron. Elizabeth lodged with Janet Donaldson in the Saltmercat. Janet was accused of lodging 'slight persons' (slight in this context meaning disreputable or immoral):

> The Magistrats considering the loss that the place sustains throw single women keeping house and harbouring and resetting slight persons, and honest mens servants and inciting them to steal, and that it is too apparent the said Jannet Donaldson uses these practices They appoint her and the said Elizabeth Hammilton to be banisht the town never to return under the penaltie of being whipt and scourg'd round the same. And in the mean time ordained the said Jannet Donaldson to be putt in prison and her house to be searcht.

A woman who was not under the control of a man was dangerous. This is made even clearer by the case of four women who appeared together before bailies Fyffe and Swells on 6 December 1715. Margaret Ogilvy, wife of a government soldier, was suspected of pycherie (petty crime) and theft. She was banished from the town never to return and put instantly 'over the water' (i.e. on the road to Dundee). Elizabeth Murray was taken up as a waith (stray or unattached) person 'in idle company' (i.e. a prostitute) and out of service and was suspected of pycherie. She was banished under pain of being scourged around the town and branded, and instantly put out of the Highgate port (the road to Stirling and the west). Sara Johnston, a widow suspected of pycherie, was also considered by the magistrates to be a 'slight person', banished on pain of being scourged and branded, and instantly put out of the North Inch port (the road north). Isobel Dougal, another widow, was also banished and put out of the Speygate port (the road south to Fife and Edinburgh).

Two of these women were widows, one had a husband who was away in Argyll's army, and one may have been unmarried, unemployed, and thus 'waith'. None of them was under the control of a man, and they may have been living together for their own protection in a town full of soldiers. Petty crime and prostitution may well have been the way they made a living, but the punishments imposed by the bailies seem disproportionate (although, to be clear, they were not whipped or branded; the threat was that this would happen to them if they ever came back to Perth). The maltman James Matthew was fined £10 Scots, not very onerous for a merchant who was prosperous enough to own horses: evidently a man of some value to the town. The women, on the other hand, were considered worthless and were simply disposed of, being banished to make their own way to some other place so that they were no longer Perth's problem. Expelling them each in a different direction, alone, in such a harsh winter was particularly cruel. What was likely to become of a woman on her own on the roads of Perthshire when the area was still occupied by undisciplined soldiers?

The accounts of the Glover Incorporation provide another insight into life under occupation. Henry Laing's kit was not the greatest expense the Incorporation would have to bear: their estate at Tullylumb was used to quarter Jacobite soldiers. The glover calling's treasurer, boxmaster Andrew Duncan, submitted accounts for the period from 3 October 1715 to 1 February 1716, totalling £162 13s. 10d. Scots. The boxmaster would be held personally responsible for any discrepancies at the end of his tenure, so it was in his interest to keep detailed records. This document includes all outgoings relevant to the Jacobites, starting with the election of councillors. An entry for 'fyve pounds weight of laundry' is an unexpectedly genteel touch that happens only once, early in October. We do not know how many men were quartered at Tullylumb, but five pounds is not a lot of laundry, just a few heavy-duty shirts: probably only officers expected to have their linen laundered for them.

After the Battle of Sheriffmuir in November 1715, the town council met only twice. By then they were worried about money as the town's financial situation had become unsustainable. During the Jacobite occupation, Perth had been cut off from one of its major sources of income: the trading of raw materials such as leather and timber from the Highland hinterland to the Lowlands of Scotland and beyond. The Jacobite occupiers brought in some money – we hear of them spending gold pistoles – but that mainly found its way into the hands of innkeepers. The council's traditional way of raising cash was to sell short-term tacks (leases) of the burgh's 'common good', its publicly owned assets, to the highest bidder at a roup (auction). Although this was a normal procedure, the number of tacks granted in 1715 was much greater than usual.

Perth's common good consisted of the custom of the town's four ports or gates (Bridge of Tay Port, Castelgait Port, Highgate Port, South Inch Port), the four mills, the fishing rights for a stretch of the Tay, the North and South Inches (as grazing land), the meal mercat, the weighhouse, the tolls of the Bridge of Earn, the packs and postmastership, the anchorage and cess boll (i.e. dues to be paid on cargo), the fish and flesh boards, and the grass of Greyfriars (the town's cemetery). The roup should have raised over 12,000 merks (£8,000 Scots or £667 sterling), but by 29 November much of the money had not been received and the council allowed their treasurer to borrow 2,000 merks (£1,332 Scots, £111 sterling) on the town's credit:

> This day the council having seen and heard read a list of debts yet resting to Treasurer Strachan by the taxmen of the towns Commongood amounting to upwards of four thousand pounds Scots money They ordain the said Treasurer Strachan to do outmost diligence for recovering payment thereof without loss of time that the town may be supplyed with their own money for answearing their present pressing business, But in respect that John Gourlay present treasurer is considerably in advance for the town and that money can not be so soon raisd as could be wisht The Council grants warrand to the same John Gourlay to borrow two thousand merks on the towns credit ...

One of the council's routine duties was to set the fiars, fixed prices for certain basic commodities. At the meeting on 29 November, they set the prices for tallow ('fourty five Shilling four pennies per stone') and candles ('three Shilling four pennies per pound'). At that time of year, candles would have been in great demand and they were evidently in short supply. It seems that the council was keen to prevent black marketeering: the butchers and candlemakers were warned to sell only at the fiars prices, and not to sell more than a stone weight (14 lbs, 6.4 kg) of candles to anyone without the magistrate's permission, in case they were taken out of the town for sale at a higher price elsewhere. The glovers' accounts show that by January the price had in fact increased, from 3s. 4d. to 4s. 4d. per pound.

At this meeting, the first after the Battle of Sheriffmuir, the council also agreed to draw up an address to the Earl of Mar, assuring him of the burgh's 'firm adherence and steady Loyaltie for restoring the King and Independence of the Country'.

The council's last meeting was on 5 January 1716. They set fiars prices for bere (a type of barley) and wheat, but their main item of business that day was to draft an address of welcome to be presented to James when he finally arrived in Perth:

> This day the council resolved to address his Majesty upon his safe arrival at this place in being brought thoro the dangers of the sea and saved from the horrible attempts of malicious enemies and a scroll of the said address being read they were very well satisfied therewith and appointed the same to be written with a fair hand on a clean skin of parchment and to be subscribed by the house.

This seems a suitably ineffectual way for Perth's Jacobite town council to have brought its activities to an end.

Chapter 7

GREAT ABUSES

I N THE 1720s, the prolific author Daniel Defoe wrote a guidebook entitled *A Tour Thro' That Part of Great-Britain Called Scotland*, intended for Englishmen brave enough to venture north of the border. He expressed the view that military occupation in 1715 and after was welcomed in Perth because the Jacobites brought money into the town:

> their expence of money was exceeding great; lodgings in the town of Perth let for such a rate, as was never known in the place before; trade was in a kind of a hurry, provision dear: In a word, the people, not of the town only, but of all the country round, were enrich'd; and had it [the occupation] lasted two or three months longer, it would have made all the towns rich.

This is certainly not the impression given by contemporary reports of the occupation. Only a minority profit when food and lodgings are expensive, and most people in Perth and the surrounding countryside soon came to resent the presence of the Jacobites.

The Earl of Mar's original good intentions are set out in a letter from Braemar dated 9 September 1715:

> The King intending, that his Forces shall be paid from the Time of their setting out, He expects, as he positively orders, that they behave themselves civilly, and commit no Plundering, nor other Disorders, upon the highest Penallties, and his Displeasure, which is expected you'll see observed.

On 22 September 1715, Perth's Jacobite commissioners reinforced Mar's order with a proclamation at the mercat cross, assuring the townspeople

> that they shall be no ways troubled or molested ... but shall have protection for their persons and goods and be thankfullie payed for what shall be desired of them.

This seems to have held good in the early days of the occupation, when there were still only a few hundred Jacobite soldiers in the town, but it was not to last. Within a few weeks payments were being made by personal credit or in 'Notes in the Pretender's Name, and [Mar's] own', 'a bit of paper, with two lines of a receipt under such a man's hand for so much meal, corn, &c.', Some of these promises to pay, written in almost illegible handwriting on small slips of paper, survive in the local archives. Once the Jacobites had left, they had no value except as a record of how much the occupation had cost local people. Whatever Defoe believed, there seems to be no evidence that many people in the town profited by the Jacobite occupation.

On 28 September, Mar entered Perth with his Highland troops. Many more followed, soon doubling the population of the little town. The sheer number of incomers would have been alarming enough. What was worse, many of them spoke only Gaelic, an alien language to most of the townspeople, and Highlandmen had a reputation as raiders and cattle rustlers. Despite the Jacobite council's assurances about payment, the towns-people understandably feared that the thousands of armed and hungry men who crowded into the town would just take whatever they wanted.

Despite Mar's claim, his soldiers were not 'paid from the Time of their setting out'. In a letter written in early October, Mar claimed that his troops in Perth were

> on a regular foot of pay, at threepence a day and three loaves, or that quantity of meal in place of the bread, which is fully as good as the pay of the soldiers at Stirling

but other sources tell a different story. According to the Master of Sinclair the Highlanders soon started to mutiny 'for want of pay', and Jacobite officers in Perth had to use their own money to equip and feed their men. Mar had too few experienced officers to control such a large number of men, not much of a command structure and no logistics. Each heritor considered himself responsible for his own men, and resented efforts to impose military discipline.

Mar raised money for the Jacobite cause in many ways. As well as demanding cess from burgh councils and heritors, he also asked for loans. He wrote begging letters that came with a threatening postscript:

> From the Camp at Perth
> 3d October 1715
> Sir,
> After acquainting you that there is a very powerful and numerous Confluence of Noblemen and Gentlemen and Soldiers, all chearfully resolved to venture their Lives and Fortunes in the Service of our King and Country, I think I need not use many Arguments to perswade you that a great many of these are but indifferently provided in Money to defray their necessary Charges. Severals have very chearfully lent their Money towards the supporting so good a Cause, and 'tis expected you will follow their good Example; all the Security they demand is my Bond for it, either in my own Name, or in Name of the Publick, or both, and you may choice which you will. The Sum which is expected of you is L. 200 Sterling, which I hope will not straiten you much, and I do not doubt of your hearty Concurrence in so meritorious a Work. You may assure yourself of His Majesty's grateful Returns, besides your Repayment; and the particular Obligation thereby you will put upon, Sir, Your obedient and humble Servant.
> Sic, sub.
> Mar.
> P.S. Since a great many substantial and worthy Men have at this Time ventured their All in this Cause, it hath been advised to use harsh Means with such as withdraw from assisting in so good a Cause; but the good Opinion I have of your cheerful compliance in this Matter engages me to address you in this Manner.

It would be interesting to know how many of the recipients of such letters responded with the requested £200, and on what terms.

Francis Stuart, later the seventh Earl of Moray, was nominally Mar's treasurer. It was his responsibility to deal with 'all the monie which came in from the Countrie', i.e. the cess and any other loans or donations of money. James Freebairn, who had helped with the taking of the town, was the deputy treasurer. As an excise officer, Freebairn would have had experience of handling money and keeping accounts, whereas Stuart, who was the younger son of an earl, probably did not. That may be why Mar seems to have had more confidence in Freebairn than in Stuart, but the Master of Sinclair did not see it that way:

> Mr Frebairn, the Tresaurer-Depute, in whose house the monie was keept, was order'd to take warrants from nobodie but his Lordship of Mar, and stricktlie injoyned not to communicate to any bodie, not so much as his master, the Treasurer, who was bound for all, hou the monie was disposed of, or to what Lords and Gentlemen he gave it ... so that our Councill of Finance continued onlie to fleece ourselves to fournish his Lordship with monie to bribe the bankrupt Lords and Gentlemen amongst us to lie for him, and cheat us ...

Sinclair, who was inclined to scorn his social inferiors and distrusted Mar, inevitably saw this as a conspiracy to divert money to Mar and his friends, although it may only have been an attempt to control cash flow. James Freebairn was later employed for many years as a courier by the exiled Stuart court, so they evidently considered him trustworthy. Whatever financial records the Jacobites kept have not survived, so we will never know if Sinclair's suspicions were correct.

Mar's demands for cess were not set at the same rate for all property owners. As with his later requisitions of meal, grain, and hay, he demanded double contributions from those who were not 'in the King's [i.e. James's] service'. The Committee of Provisions, which Mar had set up to enforce the requisitioning, evidently did not always get things right. Graham of Balgowan, a loyal Jacobite who was a friend and neighbour of the Laird of Gask, wrote an angry tirade of complaint when asked for a double amount of hay:

> how I cum to be clast with [local Whigs] I know not, I am
> represented by my three sones who have attended the K[ing's]
> standart as early as aney of the Cummatie [committee] and if I
> could endure a winter Campaine I had been there also and how I
> cum to be treated as disaffected to the K:s interest I know not my
> Loialtie I thank God is untainted ... I have my three sones to
> support with 10 or 12 horsses in the Armie I have payed ye grait Tax
> & now to be singld out as a disafected person will not goe down
> with me when many others have much mor hay then I have ...

For months, Perth and the area around was occupied by thousands of
incomers, many of them Gaelic speakers with little or no knowledge of
English. The language barrier caused difficulties not only with the local
population but even within the Jacobite ranks when Lowlanders and
Highlanders could not understand one another: English-speaking officers
understandably objected to being put in command of men who understood
only Gaelic.

Especially in country areas, where the men were less likely to be under
the supervision of senior officers, people soon came to hate and fear the
Jacobite occupiers, particularly the Highlanders. John Row, who was
then a schoolmaster at Leslie (in Fife, some twenty miles south of Perth),
wrote to a friend:

> I believe first when they took the field there was something like
> an evening (I cannot say morning) twilight of discretion among
> some of their heads, with respect to their paying what they called
> for, of meat and drink; but as to the commons, yea, the most of all
> their inferior officers, they neither did nor would pay one farthing
> wherever they went, through either country or towns, if it was
> not in Perth.

Country people who lived in isolated farm touns housing only a few
families were particularly vulnerable to Jacobite raiding parties. The
soldiers terrified their victims, telling them that Whigs (i.e. Presbyterians,
which most of the poorer people of the area were) were lucky to be allowed

to live. They drove off any livestock they could find, including draught horses and oxen. They ransacked houses and barns, stealing grain, meal, fuel, money, clothes, and shoes – there seemed to be an endless demand for shoes.

The humble country folk were powerless to resist, but if the victim was sufficiently well-connected a complaint might filter back to headquarters. A letter addressed to Lieutenant-General Gordon, which he passed on to Mar, complained of

> great abuses committed by that Part of your Lordship's army, lying at Gleneagles … they have shot a great many Sheep and black Cattle, plundered their Shepherds and Tenants Houses, robb'd their Houshold Servants, broke open Gleneagle's [the laird's] closet, the Granaries, and taken what Meal they had for their Subsistence … for GOD'S Sake take it into Consideration, and put some Cheque upon these rude People, who will certainly bring an *Odium* on our party.

The letter was from Lady Erskine of Alva, who signed herself Katherine St. Clair: she was the sister of the Master of Sinclair and her husband was a cousin of Mar's. A complaint from such a source could not be ignored and Mar directed his adjutant, Clephane, to send a sharp note to Gordon, who was in command of the troops at Auchterarder:

> The Earl of Mar ordered me to send you the inclosed [Lady Erskine's letter], and desires that so far as possible these Complaints may be redressed, and expects you'll allow no such Abuses to be committed and orders you'll take all Methods possible to keep the People under Command, that our own People may not be oppressed.

In fact, little check seems to have been placed on the 'rude People', although they may have been ordered to choose their targets more carefully.

The complaint sent by Lady Erskine, who was a fervent Jacobite, is particularly valuable testimony because it confirms that these 'great abuses' were not merely black propaganda or trivial incidents exaggerated by Presbyterian historians. The victims of such raids, and the correspondents who reported them (usually Presbyterian ministers), routinely demonised their Jacobite oppressors as 'Papists', which they often may not have been. There is no reason to assume that an occupying army of any other ethnic or religious persuasion would have behaved better, but nevertheless these events, and the way they were reported, would have reinforced the belief that Papists were capable of unnatural cruelty, a belief that was already deeply rooted in Presbyterian Scotland.

From the outset, the Presbyterian church and its ministers had not been slow to condemn the rebellion. On 5 October 1715 the synod of Glasgow and Ayr issued a long statement intended to be read in churches, exhorting their parishioners to be loyal to King George and resist any temptation to join the rebels. On 13 October the synod of Perth and Stirling, part of whose jurisdiction was already under Jacobite occupation by then, published a similar and equally polemical document which they called a 'Warning ... to Persons of all Ranks in their several Congregations under their Inspection'. It denounced what the synod described as

> the seditious and rebellious Insurrection of a Sett of Men, espousing the Interest of a Popish Pretender, opposing the Kingdom and Interest of our Lord Jesus Christ, declaring themselves Enemys to our only lawful and rightful Sovereign King George, and to the Protestant Succession, threatning us with utter Ruin and Desolation, who are not ashamed blasphemously to alledge divine Warrant for their horrid Practices, and presumptuously to call in divine Assistance to their abominable Attempts ...

Like the earlier statement from the synod of Glasgow and Ayr, this was published at length in London newspapers. On 1 November Mar responded by issuing an opposing order,

> ... to be intimated at each Parish-Church By the Minister, Precenter, or Reader, before Divine Service, immediately after the Minister enters the Pulpit, on the Sabbath next after a Copy hereof comes to their Hands.

This order forbade ministers throughout Scotland 'to acknowledge the Elector of Brunswick as King' or to pray for him by name and, further,

... all officers, Civil and Military, are hereby ordered to shut up the Church-doors where the Ministers act in Contempt hereof, and to Apprehend their Persons, and bring them prisoners to the King's Camp [i.e. Perth].

Mar's order seems to have been most enthusiastically enforced in and around Episcopalian Aberdeen, where Presbyterian ministers were seriously harassed and threatened with imprisonment:

... at Aberdeen the ministers were first put from possessing one church, then from both, which obliged them to preach in two large barns, and their people adhered to them very closely for few Sabbaths. Before Argyle came there [which was in February, after the Jacobites retreated] they were put from the barns also, and were not allowed to preach anywhere except in their own families, and were discharged to pray for King George even in their families, which they never obeyed. And had not God tristed [timed] the flight of the rebels just at that time, they were to have been put in the castle of Dunnotar.

Ministers who kept their prayers private generally seem to have been left alone, although many of them left the occupied area and took refuge with friends or family in safer parts of the country. According to William Trail, the parish minister of Benholm, near Stonehaven,

Some of the ministers that staid were insulted, and one to my certain knowledge beaten ... The prelatical [Episcopalian] ministers intruded into all the churches of those that were absent, and also into one of the churches though the minister was at home.

Mar had Episcopalian chaplains who held services at Scone Palace, and Perth's Episcopalian clergyman Henry Murray presumably continued to serve the town's meeting-house, but it is not clear what happened to the ministers of St John's Kirk. The kirk session met as normal on as 1 September 1715, but then there was a hiatus until 9 February 1716 (*see* p.151). The ministers probably left the town during the occupation, and returned once they knew Perth was back in government hands.

It is understandable that Mar would not want the local people to hear their ministers pray for King George every Sunday, but closing the parish churches was a drastic step in such a religious age and would have been deeply resented. The Jacobites made no attempt to win over the hearts and minds of the people of Perth and the surrounding countryside.

Chapter 8
A BRAVE OPPORTUNITY
IS LOST

THE FIRST military exploit of the Jacobites' 1715 campaign was a raid on a ship moored at Burntisland on 2 October, led by the Master of Sinclair. The ship carried only 300 stand of arms (i.e. muskets and their accoutrements), not the 3,000 they had been led to believe, but nevertheless the raid was successful and would have boosted the morale of the Jacobites then gathering in Perth.

A few days later, Sinclair and his men made further incursions into the East Neuk of Fife to proclaim King James, seize arms, and collect any public money they could find. Although they proclaimed the king in many towns and even in the fishing villages on the coast, they found few arms and little money anywhere and encountered unexpectedly stout resistance in St Andrews:

> The Magistrates of St. Andrews refusing to levy the Taxes thus unjustly imposed upon that City, a Party of the Rebels was sent to apprehend them; but being appriz'd of their Design, they retir'd all but two, who were seiz'd and made Prisoners by them: Whereupon some honest Woman of the Town rung the Fire-Bell, conven'd a good Number of their own Sex, and rescued the Prisoners; for which the Rebels beat some of the Women severely, put Mrs. Mary Hetherington and some others in Prison, and set up a new Set of Magistrates, whom they certainly knew would be zealous enough for the Pretender's Interest.

At first the Duke of Argyll did not respond to the Jacobite's activities in Fife, other than by issuing a proclamation forbidding the payment of money or giving any other help to the rebels. He preferred to keep his small garrison together in Stirling, rather than sending out detachments of cavalry that might be ambushed in hostile territory by the more numerous rebels.

It was Sinclair's contacts in the fishing ports of the East Neuk that enabled Mackintosh of Borlum's expedition to cross the Firth of Forth between 10 and 12 October. An earlier plan had been for them to cross from Burntisland. This would have been a much shorter and easier crossing, but one that was closely guarded by the naval vessels that patrolled the Firth of Forth. About 1,500 of Borlum's original 2,000 men successfully made the crossing in a scattered fleet of small boats: the remainder either made their way back to Perth or went home.

What Borlum's orders were is not known, but Edinburgh seems to have been his original objective. Perhaps he expected help from Jacobite burgesses there, but if so he was disappointed. The alarmed citizens of Edinburgh had asked for help from the Duke of Argyll, who sent 200 of his regular infantry to assist the 600 local militia and volunteers. They besieged Borlum in the citadel of Leith, from where he wrote to Mar to report his situation and request help. Prompted by General Hamilton, Mar marched a detachment of troops towards Stirling to provide a diversion. They stayed the first night at Auchterarder and the next at Dunblane, where they arrived late and spent an uncomfortable night in great confusion, trying to find shelter from the rain for almost 1,000 men (600 horse and 300 foot) in the small town. Although it was not very well organised, the expedition was successful in drawing Argyll's forces away from Edinburgh and Mar and his men returned safely to Perth without having to confront the enemy.

Borlum was then able to leave Leith and received further orders from Mar to go south and link up with Jacobites in the Scottish borders and northern England. Many of his men deserted as the expedition marched rather aimlessly around the border country, but those who remained eventually joined the English rebels in Northumberland and took part in the battle at Preston in November. Borlum's expedition is sometimes presented as a Jacobite military success, but although bold in conception it did not achieve a great deal.

Their early successes in Fife perhaps made the Jacobites overconfident. On 24 October, they mounted a raid on Dunfermline, only twenty miles from Stirling, with 80 horse and 300 Highlanders. They were observed by government scouts and took few precautions to ensure their security when they camped overnight. A troop of Argyll's dragoons attacked them before daylight the next morning, killing several and taking prisoners back to Stirling.

The route through Fife and across the Firth of Forth provided Mar with a way of corresponding with Jacobite agents and sympathisers in Edinburgh, while avoiding Argyll's men and Whig sympathisers. Letters were sent via 'the Hole', which seems to have been a dead-letter drop at Kinneil House near Bo'ness, a property belonging to the Duke of Hamilton that was less than twenty miles north-west of Edinburgh. This line of communication was used by Mar until he left Perth in 1716 and seems to have remained secure, although it could not have been very fast.

Communication was always a problem for Mar. Weeks went by without any news from France, and the few letters from James or Bolingbroke often took two weeks or more to reach him. On 5 October (N.S.; 24 September O.S.), Bolingbroke wrote to James: 'The person dispatched for to visit Nelly [*to go to Scotland*] has been windbound this fortnight'. This 'person' must have been James Ogilvy of Boyne, the courier who reached Perth on 6 October (O.S.), finally bringing Mar's commission as commander in chief, which he had proudly declared at Braemar on 6 September although it was not even written then. On 7 October (O.S.), Mar wrote:

> Ogilvy of Boyne came to me last Night from our Master the King, with my new Commission and Letters, the Letters are all in Cypher, which is a hard one, so they are not yet got deciphered.

The news, once deciphered, was misleading anyway, suggesting that James might arrive on the west coast of Scotland, perhaps near Dumbarton.

Closer to home, information came to both Mar and Argyll from spies and messengers who were not always reliable. In the absence of real news, rumours abounded, not only among the Jacobites at Perth but also in

Argyll's camp at Stirling, usually to the effect that the Duke of Ormonde or the Duke of Berwick had landed somewhere with thousands of men.

The weather was to play a large part in the final months of the 1715 rising. The autumn gales held up travel and communication between France and Scotland, and winter was to arrive unusually early. The increasing need for fuel as the weather grew colder was another reason why access to Fife was important for the Jacobites. Coal from the Fife coalfields, which stretch across the southern part of the county, was the fuel used for heating and cooking in Perth at that time. After the botched raid on Dunfermline, access to the mining areas became riskier just at the time when the need for coal was increasing.

The number of Jacobites joining Mar in Perth continued to grow throughout October, although desertion rates were high. Argyll's government troops were still outnumbered by at least two to one even after receiving reinforcements from Ireland. Both commanders knew that this situation would not last: Mar's letter to James back in July (*see* p.36) had enumerated just how many troops the British government could call on, although he perhaps did not realise how little the government in London cared about Argyll's difficulties in Scotland. The Jacobites' obvious plan had to be to attack Argyll while the disparity between their numbers was at its greatest. Somehow, they had to break out from Perth, cross the River Forth into Scotland's central Lowlands, and then head for Edinburgh. As one Jacobite soldier wrote on the evening of 12 November, 'I hope To-morrow will, with God's Assistance, give us a good and safe Passage over Forth'.

Above Stirling, the Forth is quite a narrow river, meandering through low-lying land. In the eighteenth century, much of the river valley was undrained marsh, impossible for an army to cross. West of Stirling on the north bank of the river there is a large area of peat bog known as Flanders Moss (now a nature reserve). Above this the river could be forded, but for troops coming from Perth that would have involved a lengthy detour. Argyll could depend on Flanders Moss as a natural barrier to the Jacobite army until it froze hard and became passable: it was therefore in his interest not to wait until the cold weather set in.

The Jacobites seem not even to have attempted to send scouts to reconnoitre the Forth valley. They made detailed plans without finding out whether Argyll had rendered the Forth fords impassable. The plan they devised was to divide their forces and attack in three places, assuming that Argyll, waiting for them in Stirling, would have to divide his own smaller forces to repel them. The Jacobites would greatly outnumber each of these smaller groups, which could be defeated piecemeal. Argyll may have been aware of this plan – he certainly had informants in Perth – and had already decided to march out to meet the Jacobites on ground of his choosing.

Estimates of how many Jacobites actually fought at Sheriffmuir vary widely: as many as 8,000 or 9,000 men may have marched out of Perth, but hundreds deserted on the road. The Jacobite army left Perth on 10 November, stopping for a night at Auchterarder and another night at Ardoch. The Master of Sinclair says the army was 'cantoned' both nights, meaning that the men were at least under a roof of some kind. However, they spent the freezing night of 12 November in the open air and in great discomfort near Kinbuck. Some of them had forded the Allan Water and would have been wet as well as cold. On the morning of 13 November, Mar kept his men waiting for hours in the cold while he held a council of war among his officers to decide whether they should fight that day or retreat to Perth.

Many military historians have written about the battle itself, most recently George Reid in *Sheriffmuir 1715*. These authors agree that both Argyll and Hamilton had anticipated a conventional eighteenth-century battle, but this was not what happened at Sheriffmuir, partly because the two armies met before either of them was completely drawn up, and partly because the traditional Highland charge, which the Jacobites realised was their main military asset, did not fit well into that plan. The famous Highland charge was understandably much feared by opponents. The Jacobites' conventionally trained military commanders seem to have been unsure how best to employ it at Sheriffmuir, although it succeeded in causing chaos in Argyll's left wing. Before charging, sword in hand, the clansmen threw down their plaids and their muskets, so the charge was an all-or-nothing tactic that left the attackers ill-equipped to fight on.

Mar had never received the thousands of muskets and other arms he expected from France, and presumably at least some of the Jacobite infantry at Sheriffmuir were armed with the Lochaber axes urgently ordered from the local blacksmiths (*see* p.59). Both sides had artillery, although the guns do not seem to have been used, perhaps because the battle began before the armies were properly drawn up. According to some sources, the Jacobite gunners had no powder or shot anyway.

It is not easy to estimate the number of casualties at Sheriffmuir. The names of noblemen and gentry on both sides who were killed or badly wounded are recorded, but no one on the Jacobite side attempted to count their dead soldiers, far less to name them. The absurdly over-optimistic figure of only sixty dead seems to come first from a second-hand account circulated by Colonel Balfour, the governor of Perth, and Mark Wood, the dean of guild, not from Mar himself, although Mar did write later that 'Our loss is very inconsidrable as to the numbers of killd & wounded'. This sounds callous to modern ears, but the proportion of casualties in eighteenth-century warfare was often very high, and Mar may have expected worse.

According to the anonymous author of *A True Account of the Proceedings at Perth* 'the whole loss, Kill'd, Wounded, and Prisoners, were not reckon'd to be above 1,200', although this may be an underestimate. A document in the Stuart papers estimates the Jacobite dead as about 800, possibly quoting the Master of Sinclair's account of the battle, and a similar number were lost on the government side, with many more wounded or incapacitated. This was a very large proportion of Argyll's small army. If the Jacobites had been in any condition to fight on, their sheer numbers might have prevailed. However, by the time the light started to fail they were exhausted and suffering from cold and hunger: some of them had not eaten for two days.

The two companies of volunteers and militia formed in Perth were certainly present at the battle. Prominent local Jacobites such as David Smyth, the Laird of Methven, and his cousin James were also there. James Smyth had been an army surgeon earlier in his career, and took medical supplies with him to the battlefield. There seems to be no record of any Perth men who were killed or injured at Sheriffmuir, but a list of prisoners taken to Stirling after the battle includes the names of Adam Grinsell, James Keir, John Lesslie, John Mackintosh, Robert Miller, and John Robertson, names that also appear on the muster roll of Perth's companies. Apart from Grinsell these are all quite common Scottish names, so it is impossible to be sure that they were the same men.

One account from a government soldier tells us

> The Dam'd treachrous Rascals [i.e. the Jacobites] had no compassion on the very Women was there, but kill'd them downe like dogs.

Other accounts do not mention the presence of women at Sheriffmuir, but it was quite normal at that time for women to accompany an army's baggage train; they acted as servants much as they would in a civilian setting. There may well have been women in the Jacobite's baggage train too, although there is no record of their presence or of what happened to them.

On the evening of the battle, Mar wrote a brief report to Colonel Balfour, the governor of Perth. He concludes:

> had our Left, and 2nd Line behaved as our Right, and the Rest of the first Line did, Our victory had been Compleat. But another day is coming for that, and I hope 'ere long too.

One of the greatest blows to Mar's military strength after the battle was that thousands of the Highland troops simply went home without returning to Perth. This was not unexpected: it was common for the Highlanders to consider their service to be complete after they had fought. For the 5,000 or so exhausted men that Mar led back to Perth, the journey took three days. According to Sinclair,

> From that ground where we paraded that morning after the battle, we marched back to Auchterarduch [Auchterarder], and cantoon'd in and about it that night; next day we marched near Pearth, where we cantoon'd another night, and the day after marched into toun.

The overnight stay 'near Pearth' may have been to allow Mar's quartermasters time to find winter quarters for the returning army.

The three regiments who were left to garrison Perth had been allocated billets in the town, and there would not have been much room to spare.

News that Inverness had been captured for the government on 10 November reached the Jacobites before they had even returned to Perth. Mar attempted to raise his men's morale by reporting a victory at Preston, an action fought on the same day as Sheriffmuir, and had the church bells rung in celebration. In fact, the Jacobite forces, which included the Scottish troops under Borlum's leadership, had been totally routed at Preston and it was not long before the Jacobites in Perth knew this.

As well as hundreds of men and thousands of deserters, the Jacobites lost most of their guns and most of their baggage and provisions. A government source reported 'wee have taken most of their baggage and bread waggons'. Mar's account of this was that:

> Our Baggage and Train horses had all run away in the beginning of the action But we got some horses, and brought off most of the Train to the place where we quarter tonight about Ardoch ...

Guarding the baggage and supply train seems an obvious precaution that the Jacobite military officers should have attended to, but perhaps the task simply was not allocated. Sinclair, as ever, blames Mar:

> the loss of our baggage might be imputed to him [Mar], for it was left in our rear, contrarie to all custome, without anie guard, on that ground we lay all night, when we could have sent it to the House of Breco [Braco], a guarnisone [garrison] we had, within four miles of us, where it would have been in safetie.

A Whig observer commented:

> the comicall part of the day was the highlanders (as soon as the battle began) fell upon Lord Marrs and Huntly's baggage and ... are all runn to the hills full freighted. So that these Lords and our Stirlingshire Gentlemen have new equipages to fitt out before they can take the field again.

Like many Lowland Scots at the time, Sinclair distrusted Highlanders. He believed that plunder was their only aim in joining the rising:

And what helpt to make the loss the greater, was the Highland-men's takeing it, who wanted no more to determine them to go streight home. They found it in the way where they past, in the retreat, who took baggage-horses and all to help them with it on their road, it being equall to them whither it was our plunder or the ennemie's, since that is none of the lead of their motives for comeing out.

A court report in the Perth archives records one isolated incident of this kind:

James Walker apprentice to Mr James Smyth apothecary in Perth being brought before the said baillie [Nathaniel Fyffe] and accused for disposing of his masters horse and the clock bag [portmanteau] intrusted to him at the battle of Sheriffmuir Sunday the 13th current acknowledged he received a horse that day from his master and likewise a clock bag of the Laird of Methvens which he received in keeping from Methvens servant wherein he was inform'd there was money, declares he fell from the horse at the part where the army drew up that morning and the horse ran off, Declares he carried the Clockbag a piece of way on his shoulder till some Highland men took it from him ...

'James Walker, apothecary', is later listed as one of the men who carried arms and 'submitted themselves to the King's mercy' in February 1716.

The loss of provisions may seem mundane, but it was perhaps the most serious blow to the Jacobites' plans. When the Jacobite army marched out of Perth, it took with it provisions for several days (one source says twelve days). One of Mar's orders gives an idea of what this meant:

These are ordering and requiring you forthwith to send to Auchterarder for the Use of His Majesty's Forces there, One hundred and twenty nine Bolls of Meal to be distributed amongst them at the Rate of one Peck of Meal for every five Men a Day; for doing whereof this shall be to you a sufficient Warrant. Given at the Camp at Perth, the 29th October 1715.

There are sixteen pecks to a boll, so one boll of meal would feed 80 men for one day. It is not easy to convert this to modern measures as the boll was a measure of volume, not of weight, and it differed from one commodity to another and even from one part of the country to another. By the nineteenth century, a boll of meal was equivalent to 140 lbs (63.5 kg), although it may have been more or less than that in Perth in 1715. To feed 8,000 men for 10 days (for ease of calculation), the Jacobite Commissary of Provisions would have had to find 1,000 bolls of meal or the equivalent in baked bread or oatcake. That is more than sixty tons, requiring dozens of horse-drawn wagons to transport it behind the marching troops over the unmade roads of eighteenth-century Scotland.

On 15 November, General Hamilton wrote from Auchterarder to Colin Simpson, the commissary of provisions:

> We have been obliged to break open the Magazine [store] at Tullibardine, as likewise this here, which latter We found empty, the Bread at Tullibardine we are giving out to the Army, for Fear of spoiling. I hope your Magazines at Perth are very full of both Meal and Bread, for if the Army should chance to come to their Neighbourhood there will be daily very great Demands, 'tis likewise necessary, that good Magazines of Hay and Oats be also provided, which I fear has not been minded much, which must be gone about without further Delay.

It seems strange that Hamilton, Mar's most senior military officer, apparently did not know that the army would return to Perth the next day, only that they 'should chance to come'. Perhaps he was mindful that Mar had not finally decided what to do or was worried that his letter might be intercepted by Argyll's men.

After his return to Perth, Mar was clear that the loss of provisions was the reason for bringing his army back there. His letter implies that he had to be argued into accepting this, and that it is only a temporary setback. He wrote:

> I know I shall be condemned by all our friends for comeing back here, but there was no help for it. I refused it as long as I could, but

was forced at last to do it, for there was no staying where I was or advancing further without provisions. I know what a brave opportunity is lost by this, but I hope that shall be made up in a little time. I am doing all I can to make us reddy again, & our friends may easily believe that I will loose no time when we are so.

A week later, reality had set in and he had come to a very different conclusion (*see* p.101).

The Battle of Sheriffmuir is often written off as a no-score draw. It may seem so from a strictly military point of view, but that does not take into account its strategic importance as the defining event of the 1715 rising. With hindsight, it is easy to see that Mar lost because he did not win, and Argyll won because he did not lose. As Sir Walter Scott wrote in one of his footnotes to Sinclair's *Memoirs of the Insurrection in Scotland in 1715*:

> To the eye of common sense the game of the Insurgents was up so soon as they had failed, first in exciting a general rising, and then in obtaining a decisive victory.

Chapter 9

THE JOURNEY IS LONG
AND FATIGUEING

J AMES WAS STILL IN FRANCE when the battles were fought
at Sheriffmuir and Preston on 13 November 1715. He was doing
everything he could to reach Britain, but the British government was
determined to stop him and to prevent the French from helping him.
Louis XIV had always supported the exiled Stuarts, and his death on
1 September 1715 (N.S.; 21 August O.S.) was a huge blow to Jacobite
hopes. The new king was Louis's five-year-old great-grandson; the Duke
of Orléans became regent. One of the provisions of the Peace of Utrecht
was that Orléans would succeed to the French throne if little Louis, a
sickly child, did not survive to adulthood. Orléans therefore had every
reason to abide strictly by the conditions of the treaty. At his elbow to
ensure that he did so was John Dalrymple, Earl of Stair, the British
minister plenipotentiary (i.e. acting ambassador) in Paris since January
1715. Stair's name alone was a red flag for Jacobites; his father, the first
earl, had been largely responsible for the massacre of Glencoe in 1692.
One of Stair's major objectives in Paris was to find out as much as he
could about Jacobite plots and prevent them from coming to fruition. His
vigilance meant that Orléans could not openly assist James, for example
by providing him with troops. Stair ran a highly effective network of
agents and informers, intercepted much of the Jacobites' correspondence,
and was often aware of their plans before the information reached their
collaborators in Britain.

In the autumn of 1715, Stair knew that James was planning to reach
some part of the British Isles and pressed Orléans to prevent him
leaving France. With a small group of companions, James left Lorraine

on 28 October 1715 (N.S.; 17 October O.S.), to begin a frantic cross-country journey towards the coast. Ships that would take him to Britain were waiting in several French ports. Although Orléans assured Stair that he was doing his best to prevent James from reaching the coast, he was playing a double game: the officers he sent to find James and hold him up had secret orders not to do so. Stair suspected this and employed his own agents to track James down. According to William Erskine, who was one of the men who accompanied James,

> they saw the Chevalier's [James's] picture set up in some of the post-houses, and they were told this was done by the desire of the English Ambassador, who had promised a reward to those who should stop and apprehend the person whom the picture resembled.

There was a rumour that Stair even planned to have James assassinated. According to an anonymous document in the Stuart papers, evidently not written by a Jacobite supporter,

> I shall now tell you a piece of surprising news, which, I am sure, will be as pleasing to you as it is to me. One Mr. Elliot, now in France under the protection of the Earl of Stair, and in his house, has undertaken to assassinate, or kill by some means or other the Pretender, wherever he finds him.

In another account, this time written by a Jacobite, the assassin is a different man or has a different name:

> ... an Irish Protestant named Kelly ... left London 19 Oct. new stile on his way to Bar [Bar-le-Duc, in Lorraine] to kill the King of England [James]. He has offered himself of his own accord and is satisfied to procure by his death for his children the reward promised to him. He is said to have received 800 pieces for the expenses of his journey, and to have spent a fifth of it on his clothes.

This assassination plot was still being spoken of long after 1715, although it was more often believed by Jacobites than by Whigs. In 1729, the Reverend Robert Wodrow, an eminent Presbyterian minister and historian, wrote:

> My Lord Ross tells me that it is generally belived that the Earl of Stairs, when at Paris, laid a designe, and hired a person, a Captain, to cut of[f] the Pretender; but the designe broke. When he [Stair] came over, the designe was disliked and he frowned upon for it; but this story needs to be better vouched ere it be belived.

James had originally set out towards Nantes, on the Atlantic coast, but he and his small party were too closely pursued. They changed course and headed for Saint-Malo, in Brittany, where they met the Duke of Ormonde who was waiting to lead an (ultimately abortive) invasion of England. Both parties stayed in or near Saint-Malo for some time, waiting for favourable winds. After several weeks, the adverse winds showed no signs of changing and James had to abandon his original intention of sailing to Ireland, or even to the west coast of Scotland. Dunstaffnage, near Oban, was often mentioned in Jacobite correspondence as a potential landing point, although this seems an odd choice as Dunstaffnage Castle belonged to the Duke of Argyll and was at times occupied by government soldiers.

It took some persuasion from the ship's captains they consulted at Saint-Malo to convince James and his friends that sailing round to the west coast of Scotland would be far too risky, not only because of the adverse weather but also because the coasts were constantly patrolled by the British Navy. The more time James spent at sea, the more likely he was to be intercepted by a British warship; a shorter, faster route would be safer.

In Saint-Malo the Jacobites were sheltered by Irish expatriates, but the size of the entourage and their prolonged stay soon made them too conspicuous. James was concerned his presence in the town had become an open secret, thanks to what he calls the 'indiscreet zeal' of his hosts. He therefore decided to go secretly by land to Dunkirk and sail from there to the east coast of Scotland, just as he had attempted to do in 1708. In one of his many lengthy letters to Lord Bolingbroke, who was now acting as his chief minister, James reported this change of plan:

they agreed that my landing on the east coast was not only the shortest but the securest all things consider'd, tho' surrounded also with difficulties so that the party was taken that I should go to Dunkerque and embark privately from thence.

It was while James and his party were waiting at Saint-Malo that the battles at Preston and Sheriffmuir were lost, putting an end to any hope of Jacobite military success in Scotland or England. James became aware of this some two weeks later, while on his way from Saint-Malo to Dunkirk. In a letter from Rouen dated 12 December (N.S.; 1 December O.S.), he wrote:

I saw last night a printed account of the Scotch battle which 'tis plain we have not lost, tho' what related to our left wing is not well explained. The gaining the *camp de battaille* is but a fruitless honor when one can reap no other advantage, and at the best what advantage can one make of even a victory if want of provisions force one not to advance; but still it appears to me on the whole by that detail that we may keep our ground this winter which is I think all. ...

James may have been reading the *British Weekly Mercury*. That newspaper's report of the battle is headed 'a printed account' and mentions that the Jacobite left wing 'gave way', without further explanation. It also points out that Argyll took control of the battlefield after the battle but returned to Stirling because the countryside afforded no provision for his troops. The report was published in the issue dated 16–23 November and there would have been time for a copy of this to have reached James while he was in Rouen.

Colonel John Hay, who had been sent to France from Perth with letters from the Earl of Mar in late October, was with James for part of the journey to the coast. At some point in his travels – when or where is not stated – Hay seems to have fallen foul of Stair's agents, although it is possible that this is a muddled report of Stair's plot to apprehend or murder James:

Colonel Hay mist very narrowly being murdered in France, takeing him for the K[ing] (being in one of his cheases [a chaise was a light carriage]), by Lord Stair's gang, and in their pockets Lord Stair's orders were found to go to such a place, and there obey what orders they should receive from Count Douglass, let them be never so desperate.

Hay had stayed behind in Saint-Malo when James's party left, with orders to sail for Scotland as soon as the wind was favourable. He eventually embarked on 2 December (N.S.; 22 November O.S.) and reached Scotland in time to bring Mar news of James's new plan to land on the east coast of Scotland.

Mar's letter of 6 December (O.S.) to the Jacobite agent Henry Stratton in Edinburgh shows how inadequate his information was, and how much confusion this caused:

> I have a letter from the King, the fifteenth of November, N. S. from St. Malos; severall from Lord Bolingbroke, the last of which was the twenty-seventh, and he belived the King then to be saild, and he had been wind bound there three weeks; but he did not sail, as I understand from the messenger til the eighteenth inst, he having seen a letter from Col. Hay at St. Maloes, to Mr. Arbuthnot, two dayes after he sailed. God send him safe to us, for which I have done all in my power! It is in the hands of Providence, and I hope God will protect him. It is not to be known where he is to land, and indeed it cannot be known certainly. Even this has not quite cured all the whims amongst us. Lord grant a safe landing, and I hope that will [sic]. The Duke of Ormond is gone to England, and I believe he has some troops with him and arms and ammunition.

At this point, Mar believed that James had sailed from Saint-Malo on 18 November and that Ormonde had landed in England with troops, neither of which was true. The Jacobites were finding it extremely difficult to organise an international conspiracy when the means of communication were so inadequate.

On the punishing journey from Saint-Malo to Dunkirk, via Caen and Rouen, James was accompanied by two of his household of whom we know only their surnames. Flannagan (various spellings) or O'Flannagan, an expatriate Irishman whose home was in Rouen, kept a journal giving a detailed account of the journey. He acted as guide and driver and evidently knew this part of France well. Mr St Paul acted as James's *valet de chambre* during the journey, but he also seems to have been medically qualified and is described as James's surgeon later in the document.

James had commented to Bolingbroke that 'The journey is long and fatigueing, but my health, thank God, is good and I can bear hardships'. There were certainly hardships, and some very close shaves for James and his small party. They spent more than three weeks travelling across northern France to Dunkirk, avoiding main roads in order to evade Stair's agents. The weather was bad and so were the back roads they used. More than once their carriage was upset and so badly damaged that they had to stop for repairs. James travelled under various names: 'I go by the name of Mr. Du Puis on the road' he wrote to Bolingbroke. He was occasionally disguised, once dressed as an abbé, at other times as a French officer. The party often ate and slept in what Flannagan describes as 'blind taverns', meaning cheap and inconspicuous hostelries. At one point, James was recognised by an innkeeper, a former soldier who remembered him as the Chevalier de St George (the name he had used as an officer in the French army) and had to be persuaded that he was mistaken.

On 28 November, James wrote to Bolingbroke 'my way of travelling … is so unsuspected altogether that I realy believe it cannot miss of being private and secret'. He seems to have been right about that: by then Stair's agents had lost track of James's party and reported that they must already have sailed for Britain.

In his record of this journey Flannagan had nothing but good to say of James:

> I never knew any have better temper, be more familiar and good, always pleased and in good humour, notwithstanding all the crosses and accidents that happen'd during His journey; never the least disquieted, but with the greatest courage and fermness

resolved to goe through what He designed on, Deligent to that degree that He was the first to order me to gett up at five o'clock in the hardest winters morning; satisfyed with the worst Diet and lodgings charitable and pious; and enfine possessing eminently all the qualityes of a great prince, with those of a most Honest private Gentelman.

It is a remarkable tribute from a servant to his master, and a great contrast to how James would be seen once he arrived in Scotland.

On 24 November (O.S.; 5 December N.S.), more than ten days after the battles of Sheriffmuir and Preston, Mar wrote to James giving what he calls a 'melancholy account' of the rebellion. It is worth quoting in full.

> Sir,
> It was but yesterday that I had accounts of your being at sea, and I thought myself obliged to do all in my power to let you know the state of affairs in this island before you land in it, so that you may not be disapointed upon your comeing.
> I had the certain account yesterday of those who had appear'd in arms besouth Forth, and in the north of England, all being made prisoners at Preston in Lancashire, which I'm affraid will putt a stop to any more riseings in that country at this time.
> Your Majesty's army, which I have the honour to command, fought the enimie on the Shirreff-Muir, near Dumblain, the thirteenth of this moneth. Our left behav'd scandalously and ran away, but our right routed the enimies left and most of their body.
> Their right follow'd and pursued our left, which made me not adventure to prosecute and push our advantage on our right so far as otherwayes wee might have done, however wee keept the field of battle, and the enimie retir'd to Dumblain.
> The armie had lyen without cover the night before, and wee had no provisions there, which oblidg'd me to march the armie back two milles that night, which was the nearest place where I could get any quarters. Next day I found the armie reduced to a small number, more by the Highlanders going home than by any

loss wee sustained, which was but very small. So that and want of provisions oblidg'd me yet to retire, first to Auchterarder, and then here to Perth. I have been doing all I can ever since to get the armie together again, and I hope considerable numbers may come in a little time; but now that our friends in England are defeated, there will be troops sent down from thence to reinforce the Duke of Argyle, which will make him so strong, that wee shall not be able to face him, and I am affraid wee shall have much difficultie in makeing a stand any where, save in the Highlands, where wee shall not be able to subsist.

This Sir, is a melancholy account, but what in duty I was oblidg'd to let you know, if possibly I can, before you land; and for that end I have endeavour'd to send boats out about those places where I judg'd it most probable you would come.

Ther's another copie of this upon the West Coast, and I wish to God one or other of them may find you if your Majesty be upon the coast.

By the strength you have with you, your Majesty will be best able to judge if you will be in a condition, when join'd with us, to make a stand against the enimie. I cannot say what our numbers will be against that time, or where wee shall be, for that will depend on the enimie, and the motions they make; but unless your Majesty have troops with you, which I'm affraid you have not, I see not how wee can oppose them even for this winter, when they have got the Dutch troops to England, and will power in more troops from thence upon us every day.

Your Majestie's coming would certainly give new life to your friends, and make them do all in their power for your service; but how far they would be able to resist such a formed body of regular troops as will be against them, I must leave your Majestie to judge.

I have sent accounts from time to time to Lord Bolingbroke, but I have not heard once from any of your Majestie's servants since Mr. Ogilvie of Boin came to Scotland, nor none of the five messengers I sent to France are return'd, which has been an infinite loss to us. I sent another, which is the sixt, to France, some days ago, with the account of our victory, who I suppose is sail'd ere now.

May all happiness attend your Majestie, and grant you may be safe, whatever come of us. If it do not please God to bless your kingdoms at this time with your being settled on your throne, I make no doubt of its doing at another time; and I hope there will never be wanting of your own subjects to assert your cause, and may they have better fortune than wee are like to have. I ask but of Heaven that I may have the happiness to see your Majestie before I die, provided your person be safe; and I shall not repine at all that fortune has or can do to me.

Your Majestie may find many more capable, but never a more faithful servant than him who is with all duty and esteem, Sir, your Majestie's most dutiful, most faithfull and most obedient subject and servant,

Mar.

From the Camp of Perth, Nov. 24, 1715.

If this letter had reached James in time, it seems unlikely that he would ever have set out for Scotland, but according to Flannagan he sailed from Dunkirk early in the morning of 28 December (N.S.; 17 December O.S.).

Chapter 10

A VERY COLD
CAMPAGNE

THE WINTER OF 1715/16 was particularly severe throughout northern Europe, cold enough for there to be a frost fair
on the Thames in London. Not surprisingly, it was even colder
in Scotland, and eventually the Tay itself was frozen hard enough for
carriages to be driven across it. The cold weather had set in unusually
early that year. Accounts of the Battle of Sheriffmuir, which took place
on 13 November, mention that the ground was already frozen hard by
then. As early as the beginning of October, one of Argyll's soldiers based
in Stirling commented, 'Wee are like to have a very cold campagne if his
Lordship of Marr contrives not to make us warm, for the weather begins
to be bitter cold'.

By early November, according to the *British Weekly Mercury*, 'the bad
Weather would oblige the rebels to canton their Men, among whom
there's a great Mortality'. Cantonment meant finding winter quarters
that would protect the men from the harshest of the weather. The Jacobites
did not have the time or the resources to build barracks, so they would
have had to make use of existing buildings.

When the main body of the army marched off to Sheriffmuir on
10 November, three regiments, probably amounting to around 1,000
men in total, were left behind to garrison Perth. The sixteenth-century
Gowrie House complex, located on the river bank at what is now the
bottom of South Street, might have accommodated one regiment. To get
roofs over their heads, the rest had to be billeted on the townspeople. The
billeting list for Lord Ogilvy's regiment shows that most households were
allocated two soldiers, but some had to find room for four or more. Even

before the remnants of the army returned from the battle at Sheriffmuir, Perth would have felt crowded with so many billeted soldiers now living at very close quarters with the townspeople.

After their return from Sheriffmuir, many of the troops had to be quartered in the countryside and small towns around Perth. Before the battle, much of the cavalry had been based around Auchterarder or even further west in Strathearn, but after the battle that area would have seemed far too vulnerable, too close to Argyll's base in Stirling. The infantry were 'canton'd about Perth', but mounted units required forage for their horses. The mounted troops were soon widely dispersed across the Tay to the north and east of the town. Some were quite close by, in the Carse of Gowrie between Perth and Dundee, but others were sent further north to Strathmore. Eventually some were as far away as the Mearns (Kincardineshire), forty or fifty miles from Perth, 'for their more convenient Subsistance'. It would have taken a long time to collect such widely scattered men together for any further military action.

Soon after the rising began, lack of ready money had become a problem not just for the Jacobites in Perth but throughout Scotland. Banks were then a recent innovation. The Bank of Scotland had been in existence only since 1695 and had only one office, in Edinburgh. The government suspected the bank's officials to have Jacobite sympathies and closed it down in September 1715. This caused great inconvenience to the Duke of Argyll, who had relied on the Edinburgh office to change his Treasury bills into coins to pay his government troops. In the end he had to be supplied with cash sent by sea from London: he received £90,000 sterling altogether, in three instalments. This was a huge amount of money, equivalent to perhaps £20 million today.

The Jacobites constantly hoped for money and arms from their supporters overseas, but in fact they received very little external help and had to depend on what they could get locally, in cash or in kind. The Master of Sinclair writes of 'French pistoles' that suddenly became available in Perth in December. These were probably salvaged from a ship intended for the Jacobites that was wrecked on the West Sands at St Andrews. A pistole was a gold coin that would then have been worth approximately £10 Scots, an inconveniently large denomination for day-to-day use at a time when soldiers and workmen were paid in pennies and tavern bills in shillings.

Much of the money the Earl of Mar had brought from London in August, probably £7,000 although there were rumours that it had been much more, had been used for generous recruitment payments before he even arrived in Perth. According to the Master of Sinclair, the Jacobite officers in Perth had to use their own money to equip and feed their troops. By early October, some of the men had already begun to complain about lack of pay. Despite earlier assurances, they soon began to take what they needed from the local people without offering payment, particularly in rural areas. This was to be a persistent problem throughout the occupation, and the Jacobites' demands increased as the weather deteriorated.

As the winter drew on and the cold intensified, conditions in Perth became increasingly miserable. According to Rae's 1718 *History of the Late Rebellion*, Mar requisitioned blankets from the local people for his soldiers. His Highland troops had discarded their plaids on the battlefield of Sheriffmuir, and those who had returned to Perth must have been ill-equipped to cope with the freezing nights. The Glover Incorporation had problems with the Jacobite soldiers occupying its farm at Tullylumb. In early November, a cart was taken, and only its wheels were returned. Maybe the soldiers had burned the cart for firewood? The next entry in the boxmaster's accounts records the purchase of a boll of coal at a cost of £2 2s. 8d. because the soldiers were threatening to burn farm property to keep themselves warm. Scottish measurements of this period are hard to pin down and varied considerably from place to place, but in Perth a boll of coal may have been about 300 kg, roughly one-third of a ton. Even more expensive than the coal was the supply of candles, at £3 7s.

One novelty the Jacobites introduced to Perth was printing. Although books had been printed in Scotland since the early sixteenth century, the Jacobite press was the first to operate in Perth. The Edinburgh printer Robert Freebairn had joined Mar soon after the start of the rising, and it was probably he who suggested the idea. Robert was the elder brother of James Freebairn, the excise officer who had been active in the takeover of Perth (*see* CHAPTER 5). Despite a government appointment as the King's

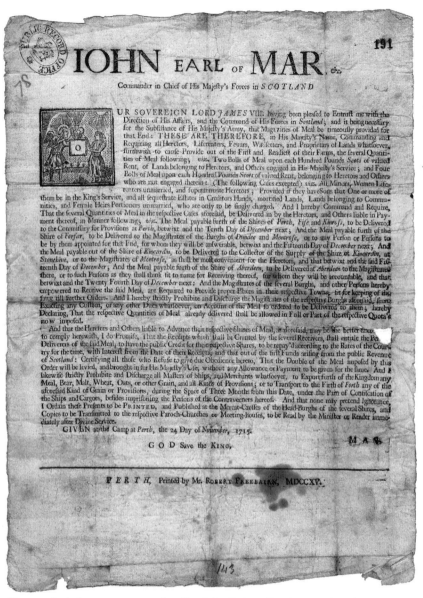

FIGURE 6. A document printed in Perth by Robert Freebairn: a handbill issued by the Earl of Mar, requiring heritors to provide grain for the Jacobite army, 24 November 1715 (SP 54/10/78). Note that double the amount is demanded from those who are not 'in the King's [i.e. James's] service'.

[Reproduced by permission of The National Archives.]

Printer, Robert Freebairn had printed the Jacobite manifesto and had allegedly been involved in the unsuccessful scheme to capture Edinburgh Castle on 8 September 1715. Sinclair, always scornful of social inferiors, referred to him as 'canaile' (scum) although the Freebairn brothers were sons of the Episcopalian manse and their father later became a bishop.

In October, Freebairn's servant Robert Drummond was sent to Aberdeen with an order from Mar asking the town council to send 'the best printing press, with such typs, utensills, and other materialls as Mr Drummond should choise and find necessary', to Robert Freebairn in Perth 'or where the army should be at the tyme'. Freebairn did not use the press to print newsletters, although that may have been the original plan. Sinclair's predictably jaundiced view is that Mar would not have wanted a permanent record of the 'fake news' he circulated as it would later embarrass him. Unfortunately, very little of what Freebairn printed has survived. Much of the output of his press consisted of ephemeral single-sheet documents such as orders and proclamations (*see* FIGURE 6), but there were also some Jacobite propaganda pamphlets such as *To All True-Hearted Scotsmen, Scotland's Lament, Confabulation and Prayer*, and *A Letter from a Gentleman in the King's Camp at Perth to a Friend in Stirling*. According to Sinclair, it was 'one Barclay, a Scots-Irish priest of the Church of England, chaplain to Mar … who wrote some little papers that were printed at Pearth', although the pamphlets are anonymous and to judge from the style they were not all written by the same person.

The press was eventually returned to its owner, James Nicoll, in Aberdeen, and printing in Perth did not resume for many years. It may seem surprising that printing flourished in Aberdeen so long before it became established in Perth, but that town had two old-established universities that would have created a demand for books.

By December, the long-expected Dutch regiments had begun to arrive to reinforce the government troops in Stirling. They were first sent to Fife to occupy Burntisland and parts of Fife that had been in rebel hands. This meant that the Jacobites no longer had access to one of their greatest necessities, fuel to keep the fires of Perth and Dundee burning. Even before this, they had requisitioned coal from any stocks held locally. On 4 November, Lieutenant-General Gordon at Auchterarder drafted an order:

> These are ordering the Inhabitants of Glendevon and Fosseway against the Morrow the 5th Instant, to bring here [blank] Score Loads of Coals for the use of the King's Army, under Pain of present Quartering. .... The Gentlemen of the Parishes are to proportion them on the Parishes.

The penalty for not complying was that you would have soldiers quartered on your property, not that you would be hanged, drawn, and quartered.

Once Argyll's reinforcements had arrived, those on the Whig side were confident the rising would not succeed. One of Argyll's soldiers based at Stirling wrote:

> Most of the Dutch troops are now on the other side of Forth and are quartered about Alloa, Dunfermline and other places in Fife, wee have taken possession of the castle of Burligh which is within 8 miles of Perth, and yesterday wee have possest two houses on the othere side of Dumblain by which wee intercept all coals from going to Perth, and we hear the fireing there is so scarce that they begin to burne their household furniture.

Burleigh Castle, near Milnathort, is in fact eighteen miles from Perth, on the main route from Fife and Edinburgh towards the Bridge of Earn. The houses 'on the othere side of Dumblain' (i.e. the Perth side, as the writer was in Stirling) would command the main route from Stirling to Perth, effectively cutting off access to the town from the south.

The wooden palisades the Master of Sinclair had ordered back in September, which were intended to bolster the town's defences, had already been used for bonfires to keep the guards warm. Raiding parties were sent to Fife for any coal or peat they could find. Others scoured the countryside of Perth and Angus for anything they could use for fuel, plundering houses and even pulling thatch from cottage roofs.

Shortage of food soon became a problem too. By December, the prolonged cold weather had caused the lade, the artificial watercourse that powered the town's watermills, to freeze. When the mills stopped, supplies of meal (which meant oatmeal, the staple diet of soldiers and humble people) quickly ran short. Even when they were working at full capacity, the town's mills would not have been sufficient to cater for Perth's greatly increased population. Meal had to be brought in from elsewhere, some being shipped upriver from Dundee. One Dundee merchant wrote to the commissary:

> I have shipped in William Buck's Boat four Sacks, containing two Bolls each, which you may deliver to the Bakers, and give William Buck the Sacks back with him, which I will take as a singular Favour, because they belong to the Earl of Panmure, whose Meal is to be sent from this in Bulk; and I sent thir four Sacks merely to make up the Boat's Freight …

As early as 16 November, this writer also comments that 'Our Bakers are very scarce of Fewel'.

At around the same time, the Committee of Provisions proposed:

> That Forty Men of Panmure's Regiment, that have been accustomed to thresh, be sent out to Dalreoch, and ordered to cast in what Corns are standing there belonging to Glenagles, and thresh them out with all Expedition; That a Captain and two Subalterns be sent along with them to oversee the Work; and that each Man be allowed Twopence a-Day over and above his Ordinary Pay for their Encouragement to work.
>
> Also that other forty Men, with Officers be sent out to Glenagles, to thresh what Corns are standing there and in case they cannot all be imployed at once for Want of Barns and Instruments, that they relieve one another by Turns, and When the Corns are dight, that some proper Person be appointed to oversee the drying and milling of them, and to lay up the Meal that shall be produced at Tullibardine for the use of the Army.
>
> They likewise propone, That all the Sheep belonging to Glenagles, Tillicultry, the Dukes of Athole and Montrose's Vassals be gathered together, and put into the Parks of Glenagles, which will be sufficient to grass them, and kept under a Guard for the use of the Army …

Mr Haldane, the Laird of Gleneagles, and the other landowners mentioned in this proposal were all government supporters; the Committee of Provisions therefore had no qualms about commandeering their grain and their sheep to feed Jacobite soldiers.

On 24 November, Mar issued a proclamation requisitioning meal from landowners, to be delivered before specified dates: by 10 December in Perthshire, 15 December in Angus and Kincardine, and 24 December in Aberdeenshire. Again, he demanded double contributions from landowners who did not support the Jacobite cause (*see* FIGURE 6).

'Making the meale' (i.e. milling the grain) caused problems for the Glover Incorporation at Tullylumb, presumably because the local mills were not working, and they had to apply to the Committee of Provisions 'for a delay of giving in the meale'. A later item in the Glover Incorporation's accounts, dated 3 January 1716, mentions bringing in corn 'within 6 mylls of the town under the paine of burning'. This order is a puzzle, as it is not mentioned in any of the other contemporary records and it is too early to be a mishearing of the orders to burn villages in Strathearn (*see* p.124-125). Could it just have been a malicious rumour spread by the soldiers quartered at Tullylumb to increase their food supply?

When communication depended on letters and messengers, it was hard to keep anything secret. Both sides used spies and informers, who used ingenious methods to hide messages:

> There has been severall methods of convaying laters privatly from thence [Inverness] overland and the enemy has almost as freqwently intercepted the letters by information or strict search, as the button, the snuffmil corke, the bonet crown &c. this letter came in the post's hand within his glove and was so folded as to answer the hollow parte.

(Many travellers would have carried a snuff-mill, which was a type of snuff box with a tightly-fitting cork designed for grinding coarse tobacco to a fine powder. This cork could be hollowed out to accommodate a hidden letter, just as a coat button could. A glove or the crown of a bonet would be a more convenient hiding place, although more easily discovered.)

Mar was surprisingly lenient in dealing with one such case:

> Whereas I have thought fit to inlarge and set at Liberty the Bearer
> hereof John Ross, one of the Posts for Inverness, who was some
> Days ago committed to Prison in Perth, for carrying Intelligence
> to the Enemy, as did appear by his Letters of Intelligence, which
> were found concealed about him: These are certifying the said
> John Ross, and all others whom it may concern, That if he, or any
> of them, shall at any Time hereafter be found to carry any
> Intelligence to the Enemy, either by Word or Writ, or, to conceal
> or deliver any Letters to any Persons whatsoever, without first
> showing the same to John Paterson Secretary at War, that they
> shall be proceeded against with the utmost Rigour: And they all,
> and every one of them, are likewise hereby discharged to receive
> Letters from any Person whatsoever, after the said John Paterson
> has perused their several Bags; and the said John Ross is hereby
> required to make due Intimation of this Order to the several Posts
> for the Town and Shire of Inverness, as he will answer at his Peril.

Throughout the Jacobite occupation the grimly named Committee of
Intelligence continued to keep a close eye on Perth's Whig burgesses.
The Master of Sinclair was characteristically scathing about it:

> The Committee of Intelligence, or Secret Committee, was another
> amusement given to some, who thought they were in the highest
> trust, and valued themselves upon it; when all they did was to
> seem useful in busying themselves in scribbling to engage some
> poor gentleman with lies.

The committee learned of the activities of government troops from
spies and deserters. They were also aware that Argyll had informants
in Perth who kept him informed of what the Jacobites were doing.
On 7 November 1715, Lord Kilsyth wrote to the bailies:

> by order of the Committee of Intelligence: Having called before
> us Baillie Reock in Perth, John Johnstoune late deacon of the
> bouchers and Alexr Wilsone dyer in Perth upon information that

the first was att Stirling and all very suspect and dangerous to the government. Therefore we have appointed the magistrates of Perth to take their bonds for their good behavior in tyme coming and to depairt the toune and goe to Dundee or any other place where the magistrates shall think fit under the penalty of one hundred pounds sterling. We also appoint Provost Alexr Robinson late of Perth to give bond to the magistrates of the said burgh to depairt this town ... and to reside at Dundee until furder order from the said magistrates ...

These men were evidently suspected of passing information to Argyll's men in Stirling. The date of the order is suggestive: perhaps Mar was anxious to prevent Argyll finding out about the movements of his troops at that time, just three days before they left town on their way to Sheriffmuir.

The Jacobites banished Perth men to Dundee, and sometimes imprisoned them there, not because Dundee was in itself a hostile environment for a Perth man, but because it was a Jacobite stronghold and twenty miles further away from the government forces in Stirling. After Sheriffmuir, some of the government soldiers taken prisoner were sent to Kirriemuir (which appears in reports as Killiemuir or Kyllymuir), an inland town that was harder to get to than Dundee and even further from Stirling.

The Jacobites' desire to conceal their movements may also be behind a news item dated 26 January 1716, just a few days before they finally retreated from Perth:

[T]he Wives of the [Whig] merchants and others ... who had been oblig'd to retire from Perth and Dundee ... are order'd to depart these Places within such a limited time, in Pretence that they keep Correspondence with their Husbands and other Friends of the Government here [in Edinburgh].

It was no 'pretence' that wives left behind in Perth, presumably to keep an eye on their family home and business, would wish to correspond with husbands who had fled to Edinburgh or Stirling. Such correspondence would have been an important source of news about what was going on in Perth, and reports were usually published in London newspapers within a week of reaching Edinburgh.

By January, the merchants' wives were probably happy enough to leave Perth anyway. Apart from the lack of food and fuel, discipline among the troops quartered in the town had not improved after Sheriffmuir, despite their reduced numbers. According to the *London Gazette*, 'The Clans behave themselves with great Insolence towards the Inhabitants of Perth, who live in continual dread of being plundered'. The image of Highlanders as wild savages continued to fascinate the public in other parts of Britain.

Chapter 11

IN 'MY OWN
ANCIENT KINGDOM'

O N 17 DECEMBER 1715 (O.S.), James sailed from Dunkirk
with half a dozen companions. Crossing the North Sea in a small
ship in stormy winter weather would have been no pleasure trip.
The vessel might have been captured or sunk by a British warship, or simply
have foundered in stormy seas. For James there was also the continual risk
of being betrayed to the British government: there was a price of £100,000
sterling on his head, an unimaginable fortune. He would have understood
the dangers of this voyage and his personal courage cannot be questioned.

The east-coast ports north of the Tay – Dundee, Arbroath, Montrose,
Stonehaven, Aberdeen – were under Jacobite control, although the
coastline was closely watched by naval ships out at sea and spies on land.
Knowing that the Earl of Mar had his headquarters in Perth, James had
hoped to land somewhere near the Firth of Tay. Off Montrose his ship
managed to exchange signals with the shore, giving the news that James
was aboard. Wary of other vessels in the area, they decided not to land
there but headed further north, finally dropping anchor at the small
fishing port of Peterhead on 22 December 1715 (O.S.). A local legend tells
that James was carried ashore on the back of Captain Park, a merchant of
the town. An engraving claiming to show James's formal reception at
Peterhead is a figment of the artist's imagination (*see* FIGURE 7). He wrote
immediately to Lord Bolingbroke to tell him of his safe arrival:

> I am at last, thank God, in my own ancient kingdom ... I find
> things in a prosperous way; I hope all will go well, if friends on
> your side do their part as I shall have done mine.

FIGURE 7. James arriving at Peterhead in December 1715,
as imagined by a Dutch artist. [Image in Public Domain.]

The ship was despatched back to France to report James's safe arrival
in Scotland, and one of the men who had travelled with him, Lieutenant
Allan Cameron, quickly set out for Perth to take the news to Mar. Two
other small vessels had followed James's ship from Dunkirk with some
men and supplies on board. One of these arrived safely in Dundee, but
the other was stranded near St Andrews and was wrecked, although the
passengers and crew, and eventually the cargo, got safely to land.

At first James and his party remained incognito, in the guise of French naval officers, although their identity was known at least to the family with whom they stayed overnight in Peterhead. The next morning, they rode about twenty miles south to Monkshome, a house belonging to the Earl Marischal, where they stayed one night. On the following day, still incognito, they passed through Aberdeen to the Earl Marischal's estate at Fetteresso, near Stonehaven, where they spent several days. The Earl of Mar and General Hamilton arrived there to meet them on 27 December. James was then publicly proclaimed king and his manifesto was issued.

At this point, James was not well. He would have been exhausted after many weeks of travelling by land and sea in difficult conditions and was no doubt thankful for whatever comfort Fetteresso could provide. He was also suffering from an illness described in the contemporary accounts as 'an ague', which means only that he had a fever, perhaps as the symptom of an infection. It seems that James took some time to recover from this. At Fetteresso on 29 December, James was presented with two loyal addresses: one from the Episcopal clergy of Aberdeen, and one from its magistrates, town council, and citizens. These were lengthy and ornate rhetorical exercises, and as a matter of courtesy James might have been expected to produce matching replies, but on this occasion he did not. To the clergy he said only, 'I am very sensible of the Zeal and Loyalty you have expressed for me, and shall be glad to have Opportunities of giving you Marks of my Favour and Protection', and to the town council even less: 'I am very sensible of the Duty and Zeal you express for me in this Address; and you may assure yourselves of My Protection'. Coming from a man who was famous for his politeness, and from whose pen words usually flowed readily, these one-sentence replies are uncharacteristically curt, possibly indicating that he was still unwell and had to cut the formalities short.

James's journey from Peterhead south to Perth proceeded in several short stages. Bad weather and bad roads would have played a part, and the stopovers gave several loyal Jacobite families an opportunity to provide hospitality, but perhaps one reason for the delay was to allow James to recover his strength. We know that in November 1716, when he was staying in Avignon, James underwent an operation for anal fistula. This unpleasant condition, which can take a long time to develop, is often preceded by painful abscesses that are typically intermittent in nature.

It is possible that such an episode was the reason for James's evident ill health in December 1715.

James and his party finally left Fetteresso on 2 January, travelling on to Kinnaird Castle near Brechin, the seat of the Earl of Southesk, and then to Glamis Castle, the seat of the Earl of Strathmore, where they were held up by a fresh fall of snow. Mar wrote a letter from Glamis, intended to be printed and circulated to raise enthusiasm for the rising. It makes strange reading. Mar starts by explaining that the party's slow progress is due to the winter weather. He then continues with praise of James:

> ... the finest Gentleman I ever knew ... despatches all his business himself with the greatest exactness ... I never saw anybody write so finely ... affable ... has the sweetest temper in the world.

What was Mar thinking? Without spinning the truth too much, he could have presented James as a brave soldier who had overcome many hardships to join his men and lead them to victory. Could he really have believed that a sweet temper and good handwriting could raise Jacobite spirits? Or, having already decided that the game was lost, did he believe his best tactic would be to bring the rising to an end with as little enthusiasm, and as little bloodshed, as possible? Who knows.

His hosts went to considerable lengths to make James comfortable. Mar wrote from Glamis to Henry Stratton, the Jacobite agent in Edinburgh: 'The King wears paper caps under his wige, which I know you also do; they cannot be had at Perth, so I wish you could send some on, for his own are near out.' Fortunately, Stratton was able to oblige: writing from Perth on 15 January, Mar assured him 'The caps do pritty well, and I have orders to thank you for them'.

When the party left Glamis, the country people lined the roads and James touched some of them for the king's evil (otherwise known as scrofula, a disfiguring tubercular disorder affecting the lymph glands of the neck). On 6 January 1716, they reached Dundee. James was greeted enthusiastically by the townspeople as he rode through the streets with the Earl of Mar, the Earl Marischal, and a large retinue of men on horseback. They stayed that night in Dundee and the next night at Fingask, Sir David Threipland's house overlooking the Carse of Gowrie, not far from Perth.

On 8 January, James arrived at Scone Palace, just outside Perth, where he would stay for the next three weeks. It had taken him eighteen days to travel the 120 or so miles from Peterhead to Perth. This difficult journey, delayed by illness and wintry conditions, seems like a grim parody of a traditional royal progress.

On 9 January, James visited Perth itself to review his troops. He is quoted as saying, rather strangely, that he wished to see 'the little kings with their armies', meaning the clans. They paraded on the North Inch and, whatever he had learned from Mar on the way south, James seems to have been disappointed that there were so few of them. Certainly, their numbers had decreased considerably after Sheriffmuir, as many of the Highlanders had gone home directly from the battlefield. The clansmen had followed their normal practice by returning home after fighting, with any booty or plunder they could carry. Living for many weeks cooped up in a garrison town was not something they could easily be persuaded to do, and the desertion rate was high. Members of the so-called 'grumbling club' who disagreed with Mar's conduct of the rising, including the Marquess of Huntly and the Master of Sinclair, had also left Perth by early December.

The Jacobites remaining in Perth had celebrated the news of James's arrival in Scotland, only to be bitterly disappointed when they found out that he brought with him only a few companions, not the regiments they wanted or even a cargo of arms. A small book entitled *A True Account of the Proceedings at Perth* gives a description of how James was regarded by the troops there:

> ... his Person is tall and thin, ... His Countenance is pale, and perhaps he look'd more pale, by Reason he had three Fits of an Ague which took him two Days after his coming on Shore; yet he seems to be Sanguine in his Constitution, and has something of a Vivacity in his Eye, that perhaps would have been more visible, if he had not been under dejected Circumstances, and surrounded with Discouragement, which it must be acknowledg'd were sufficient to alter the Complexion even of his Soul as well as of his

Body; ... His Speech was Grave, and not very clearly expressing his Thoughts, nor overmuch to the Purpose; but his Words were few, his Behaviour and Temper seem'd always composed;... neither can I say that I ever saw him Smile ... we found our selves not at all animated by his Presence, and if he was disappointed in us, we were tenfold more so in him; we saw nothing in him that look'd like Spirit; he never appear'd with Chearfulness and Vigour to animate Us: Our Men began to despise him, some ask'd if he could Speak; his Countenance look'd extremely heavy; he car'd not to come abroad among us Soldiers, or to see us handle our Arms or do our Exercise; some said the Circumstances he found us in dejected him; I am sure the Figure he made dejected us, and had he sent us but 5,000 Men of good Troops and never come among us, we had done other Things than we have now done.

This is often cited as an eyewitness description, although it is uncertain how reliable a source the anonymous *True Account* may be. The Countess of Lauderdale, writing to the Duke of Montrose, is even less flattering: she describes him as 'a tall lean blak man, loukes half dead alredy, very thine, long faced, and very ill cullored and melancholy'.

After reviewing the troops, James returned across the frozen River Tay to Scone Palace, and busied himself with kingly activities. He issued several proclamations: announcing a general thanksgiving for his safe arrival; requiring prayers for him by name in churches; stating all foreign coin to be currency (thus legitimising the gold pistoles as legal tender); summoning a convention of the estates of Scotland (i.e. a parliament); requiring all men in Scotland between sixteen and sixty to join him; and, finally, setting 23 January as the date for his coronation at Scone, where Scottish kings had traditionally been crowned.

His Episcopalian supporters were very keen that James should be seen to attend a Protestant church service, but this is one thing he would not do. A Catholic priest, Father Innes, had travelled with him, and James would not even allow a Protestant clergyman to say grace for his meals. For such a devout Catholic, the coronation oath required of a British monarch presented a problem. Since 1689, the oath had required the monarch to swear to maintain the Protestant reformed religion. Earlier Stuart kings such as Charles I and Charles II had sworn a much less specific oath, to 'protect and defend the bishops and churches'. This is presumably why Mar writes to his agent in Edinburgh asking him to send 'a copie of the coronation of King Charles the First and Second'. It seems unlikely that James's Protestant subjects, especially the Scottish Presbyterians, would have been satisfied with this less specific version of the coronation oath.

Mar seems to have been more at home as a courtier than as a military commander. He had slipped into this role with ease, and evidently wanted to look the part. He wrote a cheerfully informal letter to Edinburgh on 20 January:

> My cloathes are almost all worn out, haveing left some at the battle: I know not if you could get me any made and sent from Edinburgh; but if you could, I should be glad of it. Ther's one Bird was my tayler, and I belive has my measur, or some old cloathes of mine, that he could make them by. Perhaps he's a Whig tho', and will not do it. I would have them deep blew, laced with gold, but not on the seams. I have but one starr and no riban, but 'tis no great matter for that, a better man than I is in the same case; he has only one scrub, one which he got made since he came, and no right riban. I believe ther's neither of that kind of blew nor green riban to be got at Edinburgh; but if you could get some tolorablie like it, you send some of both. Wine is like to be a more sensible want. We got a little Burgundy for the King, but it is out; and tho' we know of a little more, I'm afraid we shall scarce get it brought here; and he does not like clarit, but what you'l think odd, he likes ale tolorably well. I hope they will send us some from France, but with this wind nothing can come from thence.

This letter was written only three days before the date appointed for the coronation. However willing Mar's Edinburgh tailor was, a new suit was not going to reach him at Scone by 23 January. He is evidently still expecting James to be crowned, but the ceremony must already have been deferred to a later date.

Mar is trying to keep several balls in the air here. As a politician he is concerned that difficulties over the oath will derail the coronation, while as a courtier he wants to be suitably dressed for the occasion, whenever it happens, and to ensure that James can get his paper wig caps, the right blue and green ribbons, and the kind of wine he likes. Meanwhile, as a military man, on 17 January he had issued orders in the king's name for burning the villages in Strathearn to impede the advance of the Duke of Argyll's army towards Perth.

It may seem remarkable that Mar – who was still in overall charge of the rising – would attend to such small details of James's personal needs himself, rather than delegate them to a valet or secretary, but the relationship may have suited both men. James was accustomed to relying on an older male adviser. Stuart monarchs before him had often shown preference for a favourite, and James's relationship with his advisers was similar: only one man was in favour at any one time. The Duke of Berwick had filled this role until he let James down (as James saw it; see p.38), then Bolingbroke had stepped in. Now Mar was at James's side, and he had to think of his own future. He knew this rising had failed, and he had no future in Hanoverian Britain other than a traitor's death. To stay alive, and to make some kind of a living, he had to go into exile with James and stay close to him. Making himself essential to James while he could was his best chance.

Mar had known since November that the rising was over unless James had arrived at the head of a substantial fighting force. Now, the question was whether to retreat northwards or to wait for Argyll and fight to a finish at Perth. Shortage of food and fuel was making life in Perth miserable, and the Jacobites knew that Argyll would attack soon. Could they hold on long enough for James's coronation to take place at Scone? In the end they could not, and the coronation never happened; James left Perth with the Jacobite forces early on the morning of 31 January.

Before James left Montrose, he handed over command of the remaining troops to General Alexander Gordon and wrote to the Duke of Argyll, although the letter is endorsed in his own hand 'Never sent':

It was with the view of delivering this my ancient Kingdom from the hardships it lies under and restoring it to its former happiness and independency that brought me into this country; and all the hopes of effectuating that at this time being taken from me I have been reduced much against my inclination, but by a cruel necessity, to leave the kingdom with as many of my faithful subjects as were desirous to follow me or I able to carry with me, that so at least I might secure them from the utter destruction that threatens them since that was the only way left me to shew them the regard I had for and the sense I had of their unparalleled loyalty. Among the manifold mortifications I have had in this unfortunate expedition that of being forced to burn several villages, etc. as the only expedient left me for the public security was not the smallest. It was indeed forced upon me by the violence with which my rebellious subjects acted against me, and what they, as the first authors of it must be answerable for, not I.

However as I cannot think of leaving this country without making some provision to repair that loss, I have therefore consigned to the Magistrats of – the sums of – – desiring and requiring of you, if not as an obedient subject, at least as a lover of your country, to take care that it be employed to the designed use, that I may at least have the satisfaction of having been the destruction and ruin of none, at a time I came to free all. I have neglected nothing to render them a free and prosperous people, and I fear they will feel yet more than I the smart of preferring a foreign yoak to that obedience they ow'd me – and what must those who have so obstinately resisted both my right and my clemency have to answer for?
JAMES R.

General Gordon is hereby empowered as soon as he has no further occasion for the money left in his hands for the subsistence of the troops, to forward if he thinks fitt the enclosed letter to the Duke of Argil and to fill up the blanks of my letter with the name of the town where he shall leave the money and the sume he shall leave.
JAMES R.

James's regret for burning the villages of Strathearn may be genuine enough, but as in his 1714 declaration (*see* p.31-32) he is anxious to point out that he is not to be held responsible for any failure, even blaming his 'rebellious subjects' for resisting him. Such a desire to avoid responsibility is not an attractive character trait, particularly in a king.

James would never see his 'own ancient kingdom' again, living out his long life in exile as a pensioner of the pope and the French king. He died in Rome in 1766.

Chapter 12
WEE SHALL
CERTAINLY MARCH

FTER SHERIFFMUIR, it was downhill all the way for the
Jacobites who had returned to Perth. As the Earl of Mar was losing
men, the Duke of Argyll was gaining them; news reached Perth
that 6,000 Dutch troops were on their way to Scotland by sea. According
to the Master of Sinclair, cynical as always, Mar's preoccupation was now
self-preservation: 'to save himself, by keeping up our sinking spirits with
fresh packets of lies, ... never imagining that the business could succeed'.
Indeed, it was hard to imagine how 'the business' could now succeed, as
Mar's letter to James, dated 24 November (*see* p.95), makes clear.

As early as October, a London newspaper had reported 'there are
Divisions in [the Jacobite] Camp ... [t]hey begin to quarrel among
themselves'. Sinclair had noticed dissention among his Jacobite colleagues
as soon as he joined them in September; indeed, he was the cause of some
of it. After the return from Sheriffmuir, the division of opinion between
the Jacobite leaders in Perth became more serious. A group who became
known as the 'grumbling club', including the Marquess of Huntly and
the Master of Sinclair, accepted that the rising was now essentially over.
They wanted to give thought to the future, to protect their own estates
and indeed their lives by negotiating terms of surrender with the government. Mar, predictably, saw these men as traitors to the Jacobite cause.

Tempers ran high: Sinclair, who was certainly not an impartial
witness, gives a vivid description of hostility between factions that was at
times close to open violence. One of the grumblers' main complaints was
they had no reason to believe that James was coming, as they had not
heard any reliable news of him for so long. Sinclair believed that Mar

knew more than he was telling them, and that James, as well as several of Mar's messengers who had not returned, must have been taken prisoner in France:

> for they knew nothing about him [James], nor what had or what would become of him; they hoped he was well, and would continue so, but that neither they nor his Lordship [Mar], they believed, expected him; or if he designed comeing, or his Lordship in the least suspected it, they thought his Lordship, by what they had told him of our present circumstances, must be sufficientlie convinced that his comeing must onlie endanger himself, without being of use to us, and required of him to put a stop to it. And Mar, being hard pressed by them, and heated, and in confusion, own'd to them he wisht the King would not come, and that he had sent to stop him.

Sinclair gives no date for this argument, but Mar's comment that 'he had sent to stop him' probably refers to his letter of 24 November (*see* p.101).

Towards the end of November, Mar sent Colonel Laurence, the highest-ranked officer taken prisoner by the Jacobites at Sheriffmuir, to the Duke of Argyll with an offer to negotiate terms of surrender. Argyll was apparently not expecting such an approach, and could only respond that although he could accept the surrender of individuals he did not have the authority to agree terms with the rebels as a group. He reported this development to the government in London, but the answer he got from Lord Townshend, Secretary of State for the Northern Department in London, was uncompromising: King George did not believe that

> in the present situation and circumstances of affairs, it is consistent with the honour of his government or the future peace and quiet of his good subjects that the rebells should be admitted to any terms but those of surrendering their persons and entirely submitting to his Majesty's pleasure.

In other words, there would be no peace negotiations: nothing but unconditional surrender would be acceptable. George I felt he had to crush any rebellion against Hanoverian rule, and had no sentimental ties to Scotland that might have softened his approach. He also resented having to pay for foreign mercenaries to reinforce the government troops:

> since they [the Jacobites] have put the nation to such vast expence and oblidged the king to call for the assistance of foreign troops, the greater the preparations are for the suppressing this rebellion, the less reason there is for listening to any offers of the rebells ...

Left to himself, the Duke of Argyll would probably have been happy enough to sit out the winter in Stirling, allowing the Jacobite forces to shrink further as more men chose to leave Perth and thus minimising the need for fighting. But in early December, General William Cadogan arrived with orders from Townshend that the government troops should press on and take Perth despite the wintry conditions. Cadogan was nominally Argyll's subordinate, but he instilled a new sense of urgency into the camp at Stirling. William Kennedy, a senior officer based at Stirling, was not impressed by the new man from London. He commented:

> ... wee shall certainly march whenever there's a possibility of travelling. My Lord Townsend by his letters seems to think it strange that wee have not already taken Perth which he thinks might be easyly done during the frost even without Artillery, but the generals here differ in opinion from those who make warr in a warm room in London to whom everything may seem very easy. ...

Argyll and Cadogan were men of very different temperaments and were not on good terms. Argyll understood that the ministry in London believed he was too sympathetic to the rebels, and that Cadogan, although technically Argyll's subordinate, had been sent to Scotland to ensure that the rising was put down as quickly and forcefully as possible. By mid-December, the 6,000 Dutch reinforcements had arrived, and regiments that had fought at Preston had also been redeployed to Scotland. Mar's remaining troops were now considerably outnumbered. There was sporadic fighting in Fife as the Dutch troops took over areas that had been occupied by the Jacobites, but Mar still believed that Argyll could not attack Perth until the weather improved.

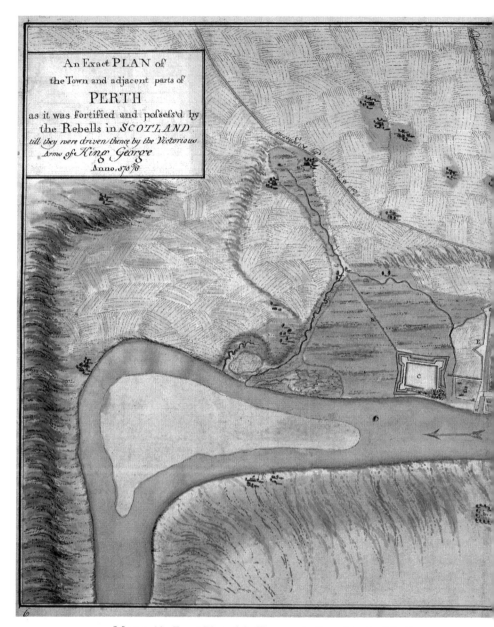

MAP 2. *'An Exact Plan of the Town and adjacent parts of Perth
as it was fortified and possess'd by the Rebells in Scotland till they were driven thence
by the Victorious Arms of King George Anno 1715/6'*, William Horneck (Engineer).

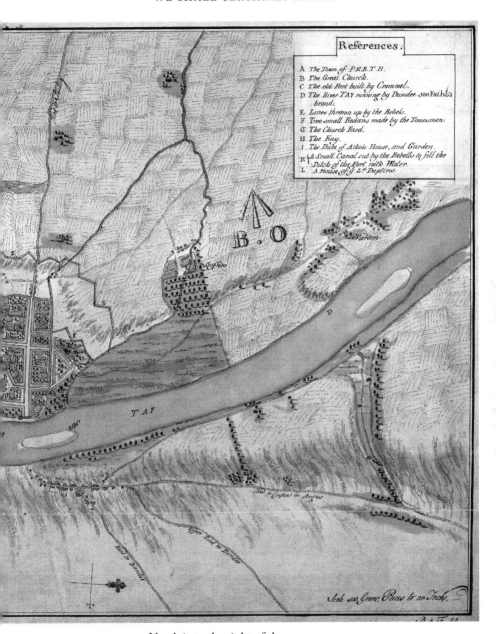

References.

A *The Town of PERTH.*
B *The Great Church.*
C *The old Fort built by Cromwel.*
D *The River TAY running by Dundee 300 Yardhs broad.*
E *Lines thrown up by the Rebels.*
F *Two small Bedans made by the Townsmen.*
G *The Church Yard.*
H *The Kay.*
I *The Duke of Athols House, and Garden.*
K *A Small Canal cut by the Rebells to fill the Ditch of the Fort with Water.*
L *A House of ye Ld Duplins.*

North is to the right of the map.
The River Tay flows from north to south here.
[MS.1647 Z.03/02c - Reproduced by permission of the National Library of Scotland.]

131

Perth was not adequately fortified to withstand a siege and would not be able to resist an attack for long. The Highland troops remaining there had no stomach for defensive warfare; nevertheless, the Jacobites made an attempt to improve the town's defences. Characteristically, Sinclair argued about the layout of these defences, which can be seen on the map produced in 1716 by government engineers (*see* Map 2). The anonymous author of *A True Account of the Proceedings at Perth* describes the officer in charge of the work as 'a French Officer, to whom [other officers] shewed great Respect, and who, they said, was also a good Engineer'. Sinclair, who thought the planned lines would be useless, describes him as 'a French fellow, who had been a footman of Beaufort's, and had takne up the trade of being a danceing and fenceing master'. Whether or not the defences were well designed, it would have been no light matter to dig a large system of trenches in ground that had already been frozen for weeks. The Jacobite soldiers were unwilling to do it, so local men had to be pressed into service: 'workmen were commanded out of the countrie, for our Highlandmen, or those at Pearth, would work none'.

From the letters that finally reached him in early December, Mar knew that James had made his way towards the French coast and believed, wrongly, that he had sailed from Saint-Malo on 18 November. Until Colonel Hay returned to Perth from Saint-Malo later in the month with up-to-date news, Mar did not know that James was planning to sail from Dunkirk to the east coast of Scotland. During that time he must have believed that James might land somewhere in Scotland at any moment. In the circumstances, it was reasonable for him to keep the Jacobites' spirits up by announcing that King James was on his way and reassuring them that their situation would improve when he arrived.

In early December, Huntly went north to his estate in Aberdeenshire, shortly followed by Sinclair. Huntly wanted to protect his lands from attack by the Earl of Sutherland, who had captured Inverness, but he also wanted to separate himself from Mar. Sinclair's main motive in following Huntly was to keep himself out of Mar's way, as he and others who agreed with him were now at risk of being arrested as mutineers. Sinclair devotes many pages of his *Memoirs of the Insurrection* to explaining his opinions and his arguments with Mar in great detail. Internal evidence shows that

Sinclair must have written the *Memoirs* soon after he arrived in France in the spring of 1716, when he was still in the heat of the moment. As well as heaping blame on Mar he wanted to vindicate his own conduct, as he realised that many of his fellow Jacobites would believe he had behaved badly.

Mar and the other Jacobite leaders who remained in Perth still believed that Argyll could not attack Perth until the weather improved, giving them time to recruit fresh troops to see action in the spring. Many of them went home for a time; it would have been a relief to be away from the short rations of food and fuel in Perth.

In Argyll's camp at Stirling, rumours of Jacobite activities were rife among the troops. Some were true or half-true; others were pure fiction. On 15 December, William Kennedy wrote:

> Wee hear that Genl. Echlen is arrived at Perth with 50,000 pistols [not firearms but the gold coins mentioned on p.106] and 5,000 stand of armes for Marr's armey, Sir John Erskine is also arrived from the Pretender with ane account that he is to be immediately with them ... there goes a report just now, but I fancy without much ground that he is landed at Aberdeen.

General Ecklin and some gold coins had indeed arrived, but the report that James had landed was just a week too early. Later in the month Kennedy wrote:

> Wee had it for certain on Thursday last [26 December] that the Pretender [i.e. James] was croun'd at Scone, and people here begunn to belive it. This day wee hear that Marr desired all the ladys might be at Scone against Thursday last, in their finest jewels and cloaths to be present at the ceremony of the coronation, and that he [Mar] went the day before to meet him [James] and has not been heard of since, so that they rekon he is deserted, and that the story of his master's arrival was only a sham story made to favour his escape; I rekon by tomorrow this will be contradicted, and a new set of lyes published.

Kennedy was right to be sceptical about this mixture of fact and speculation, but the next report was much more accurate:

ane express come from Court to the D. of Argyle with ane account
that the Pretender some days ago embarqued at Dunkirk in a
small sloop, and that there are many private letters at Stirling
which bear that he is landed in the north, and gives ane account
of his entertainment at Dunottar Castle by my Lady Marishall,
wee hear that Marr and most of the gentlimen are gone from
Perth to meet him, and that in the meantime the ladys are making
up a croun with all their jewels for his coronation.

Argyll now had official confirmation from London that James had
sailed from Dunkirk, good intelligence from unofficial sources that he
had landed in Scotland, and accurate reports that Mar had gone north to
meet him. James's arrival would not have been welcome news in the
government camp, but it increased the urgency of attacking Perth as soon
as possible, despite the adverse weather.

On 10 January, William Kennedy wrote again to his brother:

> There has so much snow fallen that it will be impossible for us to
> march till it be melted … Wee depend upon the snow for our march-
> ing, our armey has everything in readiness for taking the field.

This was the day after James had reviewed what remained of his army
in Perth, and the news of his public appearance there would soon have
reached Argyll and Cadogan in Stirling.

On 21 January and 24 January, the government troops reconnoitred
the route to Perth. On the 24th, Cadogan and Argyll went as far as
Auchterarder, and some of their men went even further towards Bridge
of Earn (which was then on the main road from Stirling to Perth). In
places, the snow was up to their horses' bellies. According to one source,
Cadogan made sure the local people could hear him complain about the
impassability of the route, knowing that this information would soon
make its way to Perth.

Although the Jacobites quickly realised that these were only scouting
expeditions, they knew that Argyll's real advance would come soon
enough. Their outlying garrisons in Fife and Strathearn withdrew to
Perth, and they redoubled their defensive efforts in the town:

there was nothing to be seen but planting of Guns, marking out Breast-Works and Trenches, digging up Stones in the Streets, and laying them with Sand, to prevent the Effects of a Bombardment; and, in a Word, all possible Preparations were made, as if they had really intended to defend the Place ...

Across the river at Scone Palace, where James and his small suite were accommodated, all was not well. Laurence Oliphant of Gask, the eldest son of a local heritor family, served as a lieutenant in Lord Rollo's regiment and acted as one of James's aides-de-camp during his short stay at Scone. He kept a note of the orders of the day, which illustrate poor morale and indiscipline in the Jacobite army:

12 January: That the Majors of Briggad give the orders every day punctually to the Adjutants, and any of the Adjutants that does not attend to receive and give the orders distinctly in writing as they receive them; Their names to be given in by the Majors of Briggad to the Adjutant General to be by him layed before the King.

17 January: That the clans concert so amongst themselves as the mounting of the guards may be done regularly that every one have their turn. ... That no fewer than 20 Gentlemen besides officers mount the King's guard of horse and allways on horseback, and that at relieving the Guards draw out one ag[ain]st another, and the Captain that is relieved leave all the orders with the other Captain, and that the Centinells be very punctual to let no Strangers pass.

23 January: The Kings guard is to be regulated so that every one may have his turn, to evite disputes on that head, which will be a shame to come to the King's ears.

Unlike the French household troops James had served with, the Jacobites mounting guard at Scone did not have much experience of parade-ground drill. Perhaps James himself had commented on this, or perhaps one of the officers realised he would notice the guards' deficiencies. Meanwhile, the weather worsened:

The same Day the Duke went to View the Roads it thawed suddenly; and the Thaw was followed with a great Fall of Snow, which was everywhere two or three Foot deep, and suddenly froze again, which rendered the Roads extremely Difficult, especially for the Foot ...

A week earlier, on 17 January, James had signed orders for the burning of villages in Strathearn that were on or near the route to Perth:

Whereas it is absolutely necessary for our Service and the Publick Safety that the Enemy should be as much incommoded as possible, especially upon their March towards us, if they should attempt any thing against us or our Forces; and being this can by no Means be better effected than by destroying all the Corn and Forage which may serve to support them on their March, and burning the Houses and Villages which may be necessary for quartering the Enemy ... These are therefore ordering and requiring you... to burn and destroy the Village of Auchterarder, and all the Houses, Corn, and Forage whatsoever within the said Town, so as they may be render'd entirely useless to the Enemy.

Similar orders were issued for Blackford, Dunning, Muthill, and Crieff, although they were not to be executed until several days later. On 24 January, William Kennedy wrote:

I'm disappointed as to the notion I had that wee should continue here while the snow did remain upon the ground; ... on Saturday wee form and march towards Perth, so that by this day 7 night you may expect to hear news of us; I'm apt to belive the cold will kill as many of our men as the enemy, but the Court [i.e. King George and his government] thinks its proper wee should immediately dislodge them ...

On the same day, evidently having in mind that the villages in Strathearn would have been destroyed by then, Mar wrote:

when they have no cover left them I see not how it is possible for them to march. We are like to be frose in the house and how they can endure the cold for one night in the fields I cannot conceive.

He did not take into account just how determined Argyll and Cadogan were to press the attack, and how resourceful they and their quartermasters could be. They had been waiting for weeks for a train of artillery sent by sea from London, but the ship was held up by bad weather. Cadogan obtained permission to bring guns from Edinburgh and Berwick instead. It proved impossible to drag the heavy guns more than a few miles from Stirling, but in the end they were not needed.

The logistics were daunting. Argyll requested the civil authorities to organise local men to clear enough snow from the roads to allow the army to march five abreast. One source states that 2,000 local men were employed to clear snow, another that 2,000 wagons were needed for the baggage train, although these large round numbers are always to be taken with a pinch of salt.

The orders to burn the villages of Strathearn were carried out 'under silence of the night' and usually in the small hours of the morning, between 24 and 29 January: Blackford and Auchterarder on the 25th, Crieff on the 26th, Dunning and Muthill on the 28th, and finally the small hamlet of Dalreoch on the 29th. This was intended as a scorched-earth policy to deny forage and shelter to Argyll's troops and prevent them advancing on Perth. Small in scale though it was by the standards of modern warfare, this was an atrocity. According to the anonymous *Short History of the Rebellion*:

> And if we yet wanted a Proof of their Tyranny, we had it in January last when by the Pretender's Orders, several Villages and Houses near to Perth were burnt down, and the poor Inhabitants thrown out to the Snow, to perish, in a more rigorous Season than was seen here these many Years. ... The poor People were not only cast out of their Dwellings, but left to die with Famine, in a Country already exhausted, their Corns being also burnt in their Yards and Barns.

There was a rumour – perhaps it was only a rumour – that the Highlanders also wanted to burn Perth before they left, but James forbade it. He also wanted the people of the destroyed villages should be compensated (*see* p.125), but the retreating Jacobites had no means of doing so. Eventually the villagers received compensation from the government, but not until 1721.

On 28 January, the Jacobites in Perth were warned that Argyll was about to advance:

> an Espress came in from Sterling, where we had our Spies, assuring us, That Argyle would March the next Day; That all was in readiness, the Carriages provided, and the Horses for the Baggage come in, and that General Cadogan was already advanc'd with the first Line of the Army to Dumblane, 2,000 Men being employed to remove the Snow, which indeed we thought impassable.

As this message correctly indicated, Argyll's main force set out on 29 January. The men were issued with topcoats and carried food for five days. In addition, the wagons carried provisions for men and horses for eleven or fourteen days (sources vary), ammunition, prefabricated shelters of some kind, and coal, not to mention brandy:

> The King alows so much brandy a man per diem becaws of this extraordinary season, and there is in the march such a number of cartes of coals to each battalion and sqwadron carryd along.

The first day they marched as far as Dunblane, where they would have found some shelter. The next day they set up camp near the burned remains of Auchterarder. As one Whig historian rather poetically said, that night 'the poor soldiers had no Lodging but the cold Snow; nor any other Covering than the fine Canopy of Heaven'. On 31 January, Argyll was at Tullybardine, where he had planned to make his headquarters, when he heard that the Jacobites had left Perth that morning.

A small book entitled *A True Account of the Proceedings at Perth* gives a detailed account of meetings and discussions among the Jacobites in the final days of the rising, but can it be trusted? The *True Account* was published as early as May 1716 by an anonymous author who calls himself

'A Rebel'. The Jacobites did not consider themselves to be rebels, and the author seems in fact to have had Whig sympathies. The book is sometimes attributed to Daniel Defoe, who is now most famous for *Robinson Crusoe* but earned his living as a prolific journalist and a propagandist for the Whig government. It is interesting that the *True Account* was published by 'J. Baker at the Black-Boy in Pater-Noster-Row', who also published many of Defoe's pamphlets as well as Patten's decidedly anti-Jacobite *History of the Rebellion in the Year 1715.*

According to this supposedly first-hand account, Mar called a council of war on 28 January to decide whether the Jacobites should stay in Perth and fight, or retreat northwards.

> When the Council was set, the Ch --- [James] spoke a few Words, and they were but few indeed, to let them know that they were met to consider of the present Situation of their Affairs, and to give their Opinions in what was to be done; that their Enemies were preparing to Attack them; and that it was necessary to consider of the properest Measures to defend themselves; and that he had order'd every Thing to be laid before them, and desir'd that every Man would freely speak their Opinion; that whatever was resolv'd on, it might be with their general Agreement and Consent, and might be Executed immediately, for that no Time was to be lost.

James had more military experience than many of the Jacobites at Perth, having fought with the French army as a young cavalry officer at the Battles of Oudenarde (1708) and Malplaquet (1709), but he had no experience of higher command and no local knowledge. It is understandable that these anodyne 'few Words' were all he had to offer. The *True Account* describes a prolonged and animated discussion with many of the Jacobites wishing to defend Perth, appalled at the idea of retreating without a fight. But it seems clear that the outcome had been determined in advance: Mar had no intention of waiting for Argyll's attack, or of allowing James to risk his life or liberty.

On 30 January 1716, James crossed the river from Scone to Perth for what seems to have been only the second time. He had supper with Provost Hay and slept for a few hours at his house. One London newspaper reported that James wept as he left the town with the Jacobite forces on the morning of 31 January. The men marched in good order across the frozen River Tay, heading for Dundee and the coast road to Aberdeen. They moved quickly; they were lightly armed and had left their heavy equipment and large quantities of provisions in Perth. According to an account in another London newspaper, the *Flying Post or The Post Master*,

> they left behind almost all their baggage, 22 Waggons, 16 great Canon, 5 of 'em Brass, between 7 and 800 Bolls of Meal, and near 300 Bolls of Corn, which the D. of Argyle order'd to be distributed among those sufferers whose Houses and corn-yards the Rebels had burnt.

Argyll's advance guard entered Perth in the small hours of 1 February, less than a day after the rebels had left, although the bulk of his army did not arrive until late the following day and had to halt in Perth to allow the infantry to rest after their difficult march. Argyll knew he could not catch up with the rebels, who marched more quickly than his heavily laden infantrymen. James and a handful of supporters, including Mar, sailed from Montrose on the night of 4 February and reached safety in France six days later.

The behaviour of the Jacobite troops during the occupation, and especially the burning of the villages, was bitterly resented by local people and was to be remembered for many years:

> Abundance of Ladies and others, are come from Perth, &c. to Edinburgh in great Distress, and all agree, That the Pretender's ordering the Country to be burnt has much lessen'd his Interest with his former Friends, so that 'tis in vain for him to think of attempting Scotland any more. ...

The failure of the rising allowed the British people more time to become accustomed to their new Hanoverian monarchs, although James's escape meant that the exiled Stuart court would continue to be a thorn in the side of the British government for decades. For the Jacobites, the 1715 rising was a missed opportunity: they would never raise such a large army again and had lost their best hope of regaining the throne.

Chapter 13

THOSE WHO WERE
AND WHO WERE NOT
PERSONALLY
APPREHENDED

F OR IMPORTANT ACTORS in the 1715 Jacobite rebellion, going into exile was the only safe option. If they fell into the hands of the government, they could be condemned to the traitor's punishment of being hanged, drawn, and quartered. James Stuart himself was a special case. He was the only heir to the Jacobite cause and making sure he did not fall into government hands was vital. His safety could never have been far from the Earl of Mar's mind ever since the prince arrived in Scotland.

James's escape from Scotland came as no surprise to his adversaries. On 3 February, the Duke of Argyll, then in close pursuit of the retreating Jacobites, had written 'I cannot but think the Pretender will embark somewhere between Montrose and Aberdeen', and he was very soon proved right. The Lord Justice Clerk in Edinburgh knew that French ships were waiting off Montrose and guessed what their purpose was. On the night of 4 February, James, Mar, and a few others, slipped away from their lodgings in Montrose and were rowed out to one of the waiting ships, the *Marie Thérèse*. Although Mar later embroidered his account of this escape by describing the presence of the ships near Montrose as an 'accident', in fact he had himself ordered them to sail there from Dundee, where they had delivered supplies. The ships had been within sight of Montrose for some days before the Jacobites arrived on 3 February. This is proof, if any were needed, that the decision to retreat had been made and the escape route planned before any conclusion was reached publicly at the Jacobites' council of war in Perth. By that stage, keeping James (and himself) safe had been Mar's primary aim. Retreating from Perth by the coast road rather than inland towards the Highlands made James's escape by sea possible, although it was not without risk. There were at least two naval frigates patrolling the coast, and gunfire was heard from the shore after James and his party left Montrose.

For Argyll, and for George I and his Whig ministers, allowing James to make his escape may have seemed politically preferable to taking him prisoner. The sight of a Stuart claimant brought to London as a captive, perhaps even sentenced to a traitor's death, might have stirred up even the most complacent of Jacobite couch potatoes. Although the exiled Stuart court would continue to be an irritant to the British government for decades, it also served Whig politicians as a useful bogey man, a reminder of what might happen if the Protestant Hanoverian monarchs were not on the throne.

As soon as Argyll realised that James had sailed, the ports north of the Firth of Tay were blockaded by the navy: 'all the ports and harbours upon that coast were blocked up by ships of war in less than forty-eight hours after his Majesty's departure'. These east-coast ports – Dundee, Arbroath, Montrose, Aberdeen – had for centuries been vital in Scotland's trade and communications with continental Europe. By 1715, the harbour at Perth had little international trade, but nevertheless masters of ships bound for continental ports were warned by the town's magistrates not to convey 'the persons, goods or effects' of rebels. There is no record of Jacobites escaping from Perth on board ship, so that effort may have been successful. Many men eventually did manage to escape from other ports around the Scottish coast. A group including General Ecklin, the Master of Sinclair, and Robert Freebairn made a difficult journey to Orkney and took ship for France from there. Many of the Highland chiefs went west to the Hebrides and were taken off, months later, by ships James sent to rescue them.

Escape overseas was expensive, an option for the elite. Less prominent rebels had other choices to make. Should they go north with the retreating army, or stay closer to home? Surrender to Argyll's men, or try to hide until the danger was over? A Jacobite soldier found in Perth, or any of the other burghs on Argyll's route north, faced imprisonment and an uncertain future. Instead, an unknown number of men chose to take their chances in the wintry countryside, alone or in small groups. The

contemporary accounts describe this as 'lurking' or 'skulking'. Understandably there are few records of this secretive activity, although, apparently,
hundreds of men were 'resolved … to lurk as long as possible, till they see
whether the rage of the Government will relent, and they be overlooked'.

One relatively safe place to lurk was the Cabrach, a remote and
mountainous area at the northern edge of the Cairngorms, on the borders
of Aberdeenshire and Banffshire. It was then a Gaelic-speaking area, in
a part of the country that had remained stubbornly Episcopalian. The
landowners were all members of the Gordon family and may therefore
have been Catholics, and in 1715/16 there was no incumbent Presbyterian
minister, so there was no Whig authority figure in the area. Although
fugitive Jacobites might be safe there from pursuing government troops,
far from towns and roads and with few prying eyes, the Cabrach would
not have been a comfortable place to wait out that cold winter: it is bleak,
and subject to very harsh weather conditions.

One of the men who was there in 1716 was the poet William Meston.
The son of an Aberdeenshire blacksmith, he was educated at Marischal
College in Aberdeen and subsequently taught there. He had been tutor to
the Earl Marischal's family, who made him governor of Dunnottar Castle
in 1715, and he was also made a burgess by the Jacobite town council of
Aberdeen. According to the biography published as a preface to his
collected works, in 1716

> he betook himself, with a few companions to the hills, where he
> skulk'd till the act of indemnity was published. During this time
> he composed, for the entertainment of himself and his associates,
> several of Mother Grim's Tales.

An edition of *Old Mother Grim's Tales* was published in 1737; the tales
are retellings of classical mythology in rhyming couplets, apparently
intended as political allegory. In *The True Loyalist*, a collection of Jacobite
verses published in 1779, a lament entitled 'The bonny laddie' is also said
to have been written by Meston while he was in the Cabrach:

> How long shall we lurk? How long shall we languish,
> With our faces dejected and our hearts full of anguish.

Meston was a talented man, but his unrepentant Jacobitism and a fondness for whisky may explain why his later career was erratic. A series of schools he started in various towns (including Perth) all failed, but in the 1730s he found employment for some years in the household of Laurence Oliphant of Gask. Few parents would have chosen such a man as tutor to their children, but the laird would have found Meston's Jacobite loyalty congenial.

Laurence himself is known to have lurked for some time in 1716 and 1717; he may even have been one of Meston's companions in the Cabrach. The only information we have about his whereabouts is an unsigned letter addressed to Laurence's mother Lady Gask, dated 16 August 1716, using the vague and elliptical style typical of Jacobite correspondence:

> Last night I had a letter from your friend delivered me by his Landlord, who tells me he is in very good health. He writes me that by reason of some misunderstanding twixt you and some of your neighbours, he can't conveniently go to your house, so seems inclinable to try this quarter.

After the main body of the Jacobite army retreated, some men seem to have simply waited in Perth for the government troops to arrive, consoling themselves with looted brandy and whisky. According to the London *Daily Courant*, 'several of them drank so plentifully that a Party of Collonel Campbel of Finab's men catched them'. A list given to General Cadogan contains sixty-four names of Perth men who had acted in the rebellion and handed themselves in to 'submit themselves to the King's mercy' in February. Ten of these prisoners were on the muster roll of the Jacobite companies that Perth had formed in October 1715. They included Henry Laing, so expensively kitted out by the Glover's Incorporation (*see* p.67). Six of the Jacobite prisoners had been among the men who guarded the town's ports against the rebels in September (*see* FIGURE 2).

Many local men slipped away from the Jacobite army as it retreated northwards through the friendly territory of Perthshire and Angus, although some of the Perth militiamen marched all the way to Aberdeen. According to a letter from James Richardson, the town clerk of Perth, dated 13 February 1716:

> There are several persones who hade accession to the rebellion
> committed here amongst which are four of this place who went out
> as the militia for the toun who tell that they and five or six regiments
> were brok at Aberdeen tuesday last and bid doe for themselves.

These unfortunate men would have marched to Aberdeen and back, a total of 160 miles, only to be locked up in the Perth tolbooth on their return. Although government soldiers were responsible for the surrender and capture of rebels, Perth's tolbooth was a civilian prison and was normally under the control of the burgh magistrates. In the unusual circumstances of 1716, the civil and military powers worked in cooperation. They exchanged lists of men who 'were and who were not personally apprehended', as the archive catalogue puts it. Second-class prisoners were men who 'only bore arms'. Among the men categorised as first-class prisoners because they had been 'active in the rebellion' were:

> John Murray of Pitcullen, collector of Cess, John Bayn, barber,
> carried arms and was made a Deacon of the wrights, Donald
> Cameron, counsellor, carried arms, and was made Deacon of the
> trade, John Gourlay, carried arms, George Moncrieff, maltman,
> carried arms, and was a common councillor, George Threipland,
> merchant, carried arms and a common councillor, James Ramsay,
> factor to the Earl of Kinnoul, headed the inhabitants at surprising
> the town, and was very active in the rebellion.

More prisoners trickled in to Perth over the following months, including some of the local men who had been most active in the Jacobite cause. Joseph Taylor, the deacon of the hammermen, was 'arrested 29 March 1716, in the country'. James Smyth, the surgeon and apothecary, 'came in and submitted, 26 July 1716'. Some were more elusive: a list of 'inhabitants of the town who were most active in surprising the town and in the rebellion, who have not yet delivered up themselves', includes the names of Patrick Hay, Patrick Davidson, Mark Wood, Nathaniel Fyffe, John Young, James Swells, James Freebairn, and Joseph Taylor. This list is undated but must have been written before 29 March when Taylor was captured. Mark Wood was in France by June 1716, but later returned to Perth.

Perth's tolbooth, built in the 1660s and demolished in the 1870s, was an unpleasant prison even by eighteenth-century standards. It was adjacent to the old town house at the bottom of the High Street, next to the river (Tay Street and its embankment were not built until the nineteenth century). It was damp and, in the winter of 1715/16, it must have been exceedingly cold. Despite its grimness, the tolbooth was not an entirely secure prison. In Mrs Moncreiff the innkeeper's accounts there is an entry for 10 September 1716:

> To 4 Sclaters [slaters] that Mended the prison where
>   Deacon Taylor Escap'd.
> 4 chop. Ale 4 rolls   6: [six shillings Scots]

Taylor may have been quickly recaptured, as his name is on the list of rebel burgesses sentenced on 16 September (*see* CHAPTER 14).

The tolbooth normally housed only about a dozen prisoners, so would have been seriously overcrowded with the sixty or more men named on the 1716 lists. Fortunately, at least some of the Jacobite prisoners seem to have been allowed out on bail. For most of them, the bail fee was only £1, with the penalty for absconding set at £100 Scots. James Smyth was evidently considered a special case. Although he was one of the most prominent Jacobites in Perth, definitely a first-class prisoner, he was allowed bail because his surgical services were 'urgently needed', but his bail penalty was set at the exceptionally large sum of £500 sterling (equivalent to £6,000 Scots).

The government in London eventually realised that trying all the Scottish prisoners individually would overwhelm the court system. They accepted the advice of their Scottish law officers in Edinburgh that it would be better to deal with them selectively. The independence of the Scottish legal system had been guaranteed under the 1707 Act of Union, and prisoners captured in Scotland were at first dealt with under Scots law. Almost all the prisoners held in Scotland who had 'only carried arms' were released by the end of June 1716, but those who had been 'active in the rebellion' still had to undergo due legal process. Probably suspecting that Scottish juries could not be relied on to convict these prisoners, in the summer of 1716 the London government decided to have them tried by English justices in Carlisle. Most Scots, not only Jacobites, considered this to be an outrageous breach of the Act of Union. Fortunately for these prisoners and their friends, the eventual outcome of the Carlisle trials was not as dire as they must have feared. Although some of the Scots prisoners were condemned to death at Carlisle, the sentences were never carried out.

Some of the more prominent Jacobites imprisoned (or perhaps out on bail) in Perth narrowly escaped being sent to Carlisle. On 29 September 1716, Provost Austin wrote to the senior Scottish law officer, the Lord Justice Clerk, in Edinburgh about three of the prisoners in his custody: John Blaye, George Threipland, and John Whyte. He was evidently writing in response to an order to send these men to Carlisle. Austin recommended to the Lord Justice Clerk

> that [Blaye] not be sent to Carlisle because during the rebellion he gave very good intelligence to His Majesty's Commanding Officers, on suspicion of which the rebels sent him prisoner to Dundee from which he was not released until the rebellion was over. Also he has a substantial trading business.

In the same letter the provost reported that Threipland, a merchant and a member of a prominent local heritor family, who had been a member of the Jacobite town council, was 'ill with the flux', implying that he was unfit to travel. He also informed the Lord Justice Clerk that John Whyte had died, although no such death is recorded in the parish register and a merchant of that name is still listed as a rebel burgess in 1718. None of these three men is named in the *Faithful Register of the Late Rebellion*, which gives a detailed account of the Carlisle trials, so it seems the provost's letter had the desired effect, saving these prominent Perth men (and their substantial trading businesses) from more serious consequences. Perth was not unique in this: an Edinburgh Whig grumbled that the town was full of rebels, but the (Whig) town council was protecting them:

> the magistrats ... put ther hand at the solicitation of Jacobit freinds to testificats or certificats ... that the persons behavd themselves honestly and loyally to King George, that they wer burges of ther burgh ... [and] surprisd and forcd into the rebellion.

Jacobites captured in England were more harshly dealt with than those imprisoned in Scotland. The government evidently considered them a greater threat and wanted to make an example of them. A few unfortunate men were executed; many more were sentenced to death but subsequently reprieved. Surprisingly many noblemen and gentlemen who were imprisoned in London managed to escape from Newgate or even from the Tower. Money talked, and some London gaolers may have had Jacobite sympathies. One Perthshire nobleman imprisoned in the Tower who did not escape was Lord Nairne, who had taken part in Mackintosh of Borlum's expedition and fought at the Battle of Preston.

> In the year 1715, My Lord Nairne & his Eldest Son were deliver'd up Prisoners at Preston, and from thence carried to the Tower of London, where for one Room he pay'd three pound sterling per week, besides one pound for wages to Warders. He was committed in Dec., 1715, & had not his Liberty till Aug., 1717 [after the Act of Indemnity was passed], being one year & 8 moneths, & he was obliged six moneths after to appear again before the House of Peers to get up his Bail & make Recognisance; so that he did not return to his own House till July, 1718. — All which coast him above four thousand pounds.

That kind of imprisonment was an expensive privilege. Men of lower social status could expect a much different kind of treatment. The common soldiers who were taken prisoner after the battle at Preston were kept in wretched conditions at Lancaster, Chester, and Liverpool, and many died before they came to trial. The survivors were condemned to death but on petitioning the king for mercy were instead sentenced to be transported to the American colonies and the Caribbean. As the *Faithful Register of the Late Rebellion* puts it,

> There were Transported from Liverpool, to several Colonies in the West Indies ... 638 Persons; who being generally of the common Sort, makes it very little necessary to mention them farther.

Their story provides an insight into eighteenth-century profiteering. Sir Thomas Johnson, the Whig member of parliament for Liverpool, offered to transport the men to the colonies for 40s. (£2 sterling) per head, to serve him for seven years as indentured servants. There was a shortage of labour on the American plantations at the time, so Johnson could sell their services at a profit. The prisoners were not all 'of the common sort'; some of the gentlemen among them argued that they had pleaded only for transportation and refused to accept indentures. Johnson had them 'turned into a dungeon ... and fed only with bread and water' to persuade them to sign. These involuntary colonists were not slaves, as is sometimes believed, but, nevertheless, they were transported in chains. Some bribed their captors to let them disembark when their ship called in at Cork. Not all of those who crossed the Atlantic survived their ordeal, but others prospered and settled in America or the Caribbean. Some eventually returned to Britain or joined the Jacobite diaspora in continental Europe.

In the summer of 1718, Whig government ministers came under pressure to gratify their more extreme supporters. An anti-Jacobite move was one way to do this, even though by then most of the rebels had been pardoned under the 1717 Act of Indemnity. The Treason Act of 1709 had extended the English law of treason to Scotland, and in September 1718 a commission of oyer and terminer was sent there, sitting in Kelso, Perth, Dundee, and Cupar (Fife). Courts of oyer and terminer had been used in England to try cases of treason and misprision of treason since Norman times but were quite unfamiliar and unwelcome to the Scots.

One of the men indicted at Perth was James Freebairn, the former excise officer who had been Mar's deputy treasurer. John Gourlay and Nathaniel Fyffe, who had been members of Perth's Jacobite town council, were called as witnesses despite themselves being 'rebel burgesses' who were in theory banished from the town (*see* CHAPTER 14). Freebairn was indicted *in absentia*: in 1718 he was living in Rotterdam, having been promoted to major-general in the Jacobite ranks. He was back in Scotland, a free man, by 1721.

The commission of oyer and terminer was an expensive and embarrassing failure for the government. In almost all cases, the grand jury refused to accept the bills of indictment, not a single conviction was obtained, and the London barristers who had been sent to Scotland to act for the prosecution were left frustrated and angry.

Chapter 14

AFTERMATH

NO ASPECT of the 1715 rising has been more neglected than its effect on the people of Perth. The eighteenth-century historians who wrote the earliest accounts of the rising and its aftermath did not pay much attention to men of lower social position; the anonymous author of the *Faithful Register of the Late Rebellion* was not alone in thinking it was 'very little necessary to mention them'. The rich local archives and neglected nineteenth-century histories make it possible to add more detail to the picture of Perth's few months under Jacobite occupation, but for most of the 'common Sort' who were accused of taking part in the rising we know only their name and sometimes their occupation.

Apart from lists of Jacobite prisoners (*see* CHAPTER 13), records are scant for the period immediately after the Jacobites left. However, Perth's kirk session was quick to get back to work. The two ministers of St John's, eight elders, and eight deacons met on 9 February 1716, just a week after the Duke of Argyll's army arrived. The session clerk added a note to the minutes to explain why the session had not met for so long:

> Reason of the long Interruption of the Session: The Rebels having possess'd themselves of this Town on the Sixteenth Day of September one thousand seven hundred and fifteen years, and made it the principal seat and Scene of Rebellion, regular Sessions were discontinued in this Place, till they abandon'd the Same upon the last Day of January one Thousand Seven hundred and Sixteen Years upon the Approach of the King's Troops under the Command of his Grace John Duke of Argyle.

The town council was formally in abeyance for longer. The Jacobite council had met for the last time on 5 January 1716. An order in council signed by King George on 10 March ordered new elections in Scottish burghs that had been taken over by the Jacobites. The newly elected council in Perth, almost identical to the one that had been ousted in September 1715, met for the first time on 6 April 1716 and one of its first acts was to declare its loyalty to King George. Unfortunately, the council's minute book records only formal meetings and provides no information about the period between January and April.

In Dundee, the Duke of Argyll had appointed an interim council of men loyal to King George on the day his army arrived (3 February), under a military governor. He probably did the same in Perth, as Provost Austin and other councillors who had been ousted in September 1715 seem to have returned to the town very soon after the Jacobites had left.

Just like their Jacobite predecessors the newly installed Whig town council had urgent financial problems. In April 1716, the council rouped (i.e. auctioned) the town's common good for six months, raising over 10,000 merks (£6,666 Scots). The men who had invested in the Jacobite roup back in October 1715 (*see* p.71) had not fared well: some of them had received little or no income from their investment. The Jacobite troops had paid no dues at the ports or the harbour, and the cold weather had soon prevented use of the river for navigation or fishing as well as stopping the mills. Despite this, on 23 April 1716, the council ordered John Duff and James Inglis, 'pretended tacksmen of the milns during the time of the late rebellion' to pay £1,000 Scots to the burgh treasurer, although it is not clear whether they ever did pay this penalty. The men who bid for the common good in April 1716 would have a better chance of getting some return on their money as the weather improved and the town's commerce got going again.

The reinstated council also had to deal with urgent repair work, such as the filling in of trenches, and numerous claims for reparations. Much of the town's grazing land had been rendered unusable by military activity, and other property belonging to the town had been damaged during the occupation. The tacksmen to whom it was leased out petitioned for remission of cess. Perhaps the most unusual petition was one from

Agnes Rankin, asking for 'encouragement' of her girls' school, 'which was putt much out of its course by the late Rebellion'. The council also had to deal with Perth's Jacobite citizens, always referred to in the official records as 'rebel burgesses'. When men became burgesses of Perth, they swore an oath to uphold the Protestant religion, to be 'leal and true' to the reigning monarch and his or her successors, and to obey the laws and statutes of the burgh. In September 1716, the rebel burgesses were charged with breaking the 'sacred ty and obligation of their Burgess Oath'. Adding the sin of oath-breaking to the crime of armed rebellion made it much more serious – this is why the rising was often described as 'wicked' rebellion.

The rebel burgesses were not sentenced until September 1716. Eighty-three of them were named in a lengthy proclamation read out at the mercat cross on 16 September. They were condemned by the magistrates as rebels, 'having shaken off the fear of God, all regaird to His Majesty's Laws, the Laws and Constitutions of this Burgh and the sacred ty and obligation of their Burgess Oath'. They were condemned to

> Remove themselves further off and from this Burgh, betwixt [now] and the term of Martinmas next 1716 and never to return thereto after the said term, Each of them under the penalty of Two hundered pounds Scots money in case of failure at their performance.

Their burgess tickets were torn up to demonstrate their loss of burgess status. Banishment and loss of burgess status meant in theory that these men would have no way of earning a living because they could not legally follow their trade or profession. However, it is one thing to pronounce a sentence and another to enforce it, as the council was to find. The sentence of banishment and the severe penalties seem to have had little effect, as the magistrates had apparently turned a blind eye:

> The Magistrates however have been so mild in the Execution of their sentence, That all those contain'd in it, who had given the least Evidence of their future Loyalty to his Majestie, have been allowed to reside in the town and Exerce their Employment as if no such sentence had past against them.

Many Jacobite supporters neither left the town nor paid the fine, and it would be years before the legal arguments were settled.

The town council of Perth had authority over the burgh and its inhabitants, but not over the rest of Perthshire, a county that was home to many heritor families who had either actively supported the Jacobites or sympathised with them. By early 1716, the lord lieutenant of the county, the Duke of Atholl, was in residence at Huntingtower Castle (*see* FIGURE 3), just west of Perth. His wife and family were with him. Not all of his family, of course: three of his older sons, including his heir, had joined the rebels, and gone into exile. But he had young children by his second wife; in fact, she had given birth to a son as recently as 8 January 1716. Atholl had been the sheriff of Perthshire since 1695 and was appointed lord lieutenant in 1715. In addition to his status as the most important local nobleman, he thus embodied the power of King George in Perthshire. As lord lieutenant, he was the monarch's personal representative and controlled the militia, and as sheriff he was responsible for royal justice.

In peacetime, these might have been largely honorary roles, deputed to subordinates, but in February 1716, Atholl's presence provided a focus of civilian government. On 13 February 1716, James Richardson, the town clerk of Perth, wrote, 'the Duke of Atholl is at huntingtour on the bussieness of his Lieutenancy and I'm obliedged to more than ordinary attendance there…', implying that the town clerk (a paid official) had to liaise between the town council and the duke.

In June 1716, parliament passed 'An Act for the more Effectual Securing the Peace of the Highlands in Scotland', usually known as the Disarming Act, which came into force on 1 November 1716. Among other measures, it prohibited the bearing of arms throughout all of Scotland north of Stirling, which included Perth itself and the whole of Perthshire. Another provision of the Disarming Act was 'That the Arms in Burghs Royal be kept in Magazines under the Care of the Magistrates and not left in private Houses'. In the Perth archives, there is a record dated 10 October 1716 of 'Persons who gave in such of the town's arms as were in their custody in obedience to the Magistrate's order', presumably in response to this Act. Sixteen men (including Provost Austin) handed in weapons: fifteen firelocks, two of which were damaged; four 'carribanes' [carbines]; one fowling piece; and two bayonets. This seems an implausibly small total for a town so recently occupied by thousands of men under arms. The reluctance to hand in weapons may simply reflect a desire to be prepared if civil war broke out again, or perhaps the understandable resentment of Perth's Whig loyalists towards a law that treated them as if they were potential rebels.

Many of the Jacobite soldiers, the 'men who had only carried arms', claimed that they had been forced out by threats from their landlords, such as those issued by the Earl of Mar in September 1715:

> let my own tenants in Kildrummy know, that if they come not forth with their best arms, I will send a party immediately to burn what they shall miss taking from them ...

The Disarming Act stripped heritors of these feudal powers:

> Whereas the prevailing Custom of convocating Numbers of His Majesty's Subjects together with the Practice of obliging them to perform divers Services Arbitrary and Oppressive, by Virtue of Clauses in Charters, Contracts, or Agreements, within the Limits aforesaid, is contrary to the Nature of good Government, destructive of the Liberties of Free People, inconsistent with the Obedience and Allegiance due to His Majesty and Government, as well as the greatest Obstruction to the Improvement of Trade, Husbandry, and Manufactories, and was one of the greatest Means of raising and carrying on the late unhappy Rebellion.

In 1717, parliament passed 'An Act for the Kings most Gracious, General, and Free Pardon', generally known as the Indemnity Act. Despite its name, the pardon did not cover everyone or everything: the printed version of the act has three pages of pardon and eleven pages of general and specific exceptions. It excluded some Jacobites by name, including anyone called Macgregor, as well as all those who were fugitives from justice or had already gone to join James in exile. The Indemnity Act allowed most of the men who had been living in hiding (*see* CHAPTER 13) to resume their normal life in safety.

In Perth, the sentences against the former burgesses were renewed after the 1717 Indemnity Act. Legal arguments continued at the Court of Session in Edinburgh, the legal documents got longer and longer, and the legal bills on both sides would have mounted up. In 1718, four of the rebel burgesses – ex-Provost Patrick Davidson, James Smyth, John Paterson, and James Swells – petitioned the provost and magistrates of Perth stating that 'following the King's Indemnity the council's sentence had been suspended by the Court of Session, and they now wished to live as friends with the Council'. The council responded that they had a duty to protect the town:

> now that they are threaten'd with an invasion and a new Rebellion [the abortive 1719 attempt on the west coast], and have good reason to believe that Mr Davidson and some other of his Accomplices will at this Juncture use their utmost efforts to Delude the Inhabitants to Act the same Game over again, unless he be prevented.

Eventually, the council made a serious effort to collect the fines, at least from the men who could afford to pay. On 17 March 1719, there was a court order for 'the arrestment and pounding [confiscation] of goods of former Perth burgesses Patrick Davidson, James Swells, Joseph Taylor, Henry Murray, and M[ess]rs John & William Paterson, for defying the court order to pay £200 Scots'. There, unfortunately, the story peters out: it is not clear whether the fines were eventually paid, or whether Davidson and the others were allowed to 'live as friends' with the council. The important point is that they did not regain their burgess privileges, unlike Jacobites in some other burghs such as Aberdeen. Memories were long: in 1726, some members of Perth's Hammermen Corporation complained that William Cargill (elder and younger), Joseph Taylor, James Cheape, John Petersone [Paterson] and Charles Elder – all known Jacobites – had been permitted to vote at a meeting, although in October 1719 the town council had expressly forbidden them to take part in any proceedings of the Guildry and trades.

Why did the town council pursue this legal point so relentlessly? Provost Austin had prevented captured Jacobites being extradited to

Carlisle, so personal vindictiveness does not seem to be the motive. The answer must lie in the constitution of the royal burgh of Perth. The Jacobites who helped Hay to take Perth in September 1715 were Episcopalian Tories from elite local families who had been out of power in the burgh since the Revolution of 1689. Depriving these men of their burgess status as a punishment had political as well as economic implications. Although the council had allowed the ex-burgesses to carry on their occupations in the town, only burgesses could become councillors. Because the parliamentary franchise in Scottish burghs at that time was limited to councillors, the former burgesses had no role in national government either. It would have been only natural for these men to resent their political emasculation and welcome the opportunity for redress when it finally came. Their Jacobite identity was almost all they had left, so perhaps that is why they were prepared, apparently against all common sense, to fight for it again in 1745.

Episcopalianism remained an important part of Jacobite identity. Episcopalian clergymen prudently went into hiding in 1716, but at least one, Thomas Murray, was reported to be active around Perth in 1717 and 1718. Despite a harsh 1719 law restricting their public worship, as well as internal doctrinal divisions, the Episcopalians re-established an episcopal hierarchy in the 1720s and once again provided a focus for Jacobite sympathisers. The newly installed hierarchy was firmly linked to the exiled James Stuart, who acted as head of the church by nominating bishops; a fact not mentioned in a recent history of the Episcopal Church of Scotland, which says little about the Jacobite connection.

Accounts of the aftermath of the 1715 rebellion often tend to give the impression that once the rebels had disbanded, peace was soon restored in a gentlemanly way. This seems to be largely true for the elite landed families, the heritors, but perhaps not for other sectors of the population. Heritor families were closely linked by bonds of cousinhood and marriage, and almost all of them would have had some family member or friend involved in the rebellion. They also had estates and other assets they wished to protect, and the government knew that the most effective punishment for them would be to deprive them and their successors of these assets. George I had announced in January 1716 that he intended to use forfeited estates to defray the cost of putting down the rising, rather than increasing the burden on loyal taxpayers:

> Among the many unavoidable ill Consequences of this Rebellion, none affects more sensibly, than that extraordinary Burden, which it has, and must create to my faithful Subjects. To ease them as far as lies in my Power, I take this first Opportunity of Declaring, That I will freely give up all the Estates, that shall become forfeited to the Crown by this Rebellion, to be applied towards defraying the Extraordinary Expence, incurr'd on this Occasion.

It is sometimes forgotten that before he came to the throne of Great Britain, George had many years of experience as a soldier and as ruler of Hanover. He knew the costs of making war, and also the unpopularity of taxes.

The Jacobites' often successful efforts to bamboozle the Commission for Forfeited Estates set up by the government have left a paper trail; so have the accounts of their imprisonment and trial, and often their eventual pardon. Although impoverished by legal fees and bribes, the heritors soon managed to pick up the dropped stitches of the social fabric. It is not so easy to get any idea of what happened to people below this elite level. It would be a mistake to assume there was no continuing ill feeling between Jacobites and Whigs; examples throughout history tell us that civil strife rarely ends with a polite handshake. Perth itself was governed by Whig magistrates and also garrisoned by government soldiers, so it is unlikely that there would be overt Jacobite violence within the burgh itself. In remoter parts of rural Scotland that were traditionally Episcopalian strongholds, from Perthshire to Speyside, Presbyterian ministers and isolated Whigs were harassed and sometimes beaten up by Jacobite sympathisers.

The 1715 rising was not a decisive event. Its outcome confirmed what most people already realised, and what the Jacobites used as an excuse for its failure, that no attempt to overthrow the Hanoverian dynasty could succeed without substantial help from outside. Modern historians describe Scotland in the early eighteenth century as being a society in the process of relatively rapid change. A Whig view of the rising might see it as merely a step in this change, one of the growing pains of the new United Kingdom. Alternatively, we could see it as a rebellion against decades of neglect by a central government in London that knew little and cared less about far-flung parts of the realm.

For many of Perth's townspeople, it may not have made much difference who sat on the throne or even in the council seats. The fact that the council and the Guildry together did not find it easy to enlist enough men to form two companies of Jacobite soldiers, and that some of the men who eventually signed up were the same ones who had earlier been paid by the Whig council to guard the town's gates, indicates that there was no special enthusiasm for a Jacobite rising among the poorer people of the town. Although its outcome determined who would govern Perth and the other Scottish burghs and who would represent them in parliament for at least a generation, to the people of Perth the 1715 rising may have seemed like just one more armed incursion in a series of such events that had been going on since medieval times. They were not to know that it would be almost the last such upheaval.

Military activities such as the construction of roads eventually helped the town's economy, but Perth did not prosper until later in the eighteenth century when the textile trade began to flourish. The 1715 rising was not a revolution: it did not change the structure of government. The 'Liberties of Free People' and the 'Improvement of Trade, Husbandry, and Manufactories', so boldly proclaimed in the Disarming Act of 1716, were only on the distant horizon.

BRIEF
BIOGRAPHIES

James Butler, 2nd Duke of Ormonde (1665–1745)

ORMONDE had considerable military experience, campaigning in Europe with William III in the 1690s and attaining the rank of lieutenant-general. In 1712, after the dismissal of the Duke of Marlborough, he was appointed commander-in-chief of the armed forces in England and captain-general. However, he seems to have been a dubious asset to the Jacobite cause. Generous and extravagant by nature, he was not cut out to be a conspirator. According to Bolingbroke he was 'honest, brave, popular and willing, but must be guided by some wise people' and James later noted '[o]ur good hearty Duke wants a good head with him'. He fled to Paris in August 1715, disrupting plans for a Jacobite rising in the west of England, and took no further active part in Jacobite affairs.

John Campbell, 2nd Duke of Argyll (1680–1743)

ARGYLL served under Marlborough in the War of the Spanish Succession and was appointed Commander-in-Chief, Scotland in 1712. After 1715, he was not fully trusted by the Whig government, who considered him to be insufficiently decisive in dealing with the rising and perhaps not fully committed to the Hanoverian succession. Although his subsequent career suffered from political setbacks, he was eventually promoted to field-marshal.

John Dalrymple, 1st Earl of Stair (1648–1707)

AS A SENIOR MEMBER of James VII's administration in Scotland, Stair became unpopular both with Jacobites and with supporters of the Williamite regime. He played a key role in suppressing the 1689–92 Jacobite rising and was forced to resign in 1695 for his responsibility in organising the massacre of Glencoe.

John Dalrymple, 2nd Earl of Stair (1673–1747)

IN JANUARY 1715, Stair was appointed minister plenipotentiary at Paris. He made friends with the Duke of Orléans, who became regent on the death of Louis XIV, keeping a close watch to ensure that the French abided by the terms of the Peace of Utrecht. Stair's greatest service to British interests was his success in combatting the threat of Jacobitism. He ran an effective intelligence service that kept him informed of Jacobite intrigues and kept covert French assistance to them in check.

James Drummond, 4th Earl of Perth (1648–1716)

DRUMMOND and his brother Lord Melfort had converted to Catholicism in 1685. The earl was one of the most important landowners in Perthshire, with estates at Drummond Castle near Crieff and at Stobhall a few miles north of Perth. The Perth council records refer to 'Popish worship' at Stobhall in the 1680s, and in 1700 Drummond Castle became an official Catholic mission station and a nucleus of Catholic worship in Perthshire. Lord Perth died in exile at St Germain in 1716. His son and heir, Lord Drummond, led the attempt on Edinburgh Castle in September 1715 and commanded the cavalry at the Battle of Sheriffmuir. He escaped from Montrose in February 1716 with James, Mar, and his cousin, the 2nd Lord Melfort.

John Erskine, Earl of Mar,
and Jacobite Duke of Mar (1675–1732)

MAR succeeded his father in May 1689 and took his seat in the Scottish parliament in September 1696. He inherited heavily indebted estates and depended on political office for his income. Until 1714 he was in government office, first in Scotland and then after 1707 in England. He came to prominence in London during the negotiations for the Treaty of Union. He was elected one of the sixteen representative peers of Scotland at Westminster and in 1713 was appointed secretary of state for Scotland. Despite his Scottish Episcopalian background and Tory politics, he had not demonstrated any obvious sympathy for the Jacobite cause before George I's accession. After fleeing to France with James in February 1716, he soon succeeded Lord Bolingbroke as the Jacobite secretary of state.

He kept in touch with Whigs in Britain and became essentially a double agent, providing information to George I until James dismissed him in 1724. By the late 1720s, Mar was living in Paris with his family, with occasional payments from the British government as their only financial support. His wife's mental health gave way and she was brought back to England by her sister Lady Mary Wortley Montague. In 1729, Mar left Paris to avoid his creditors and moved to the Low Countries where life was cheaper. He died at Aix-la-Chapelle in 1732.

James Fitzjames, 1st Duke of Berwick (1670–1734)

BERWICK was the illegitimate son of James II by his mistress Arabella Churchill, sister of the Duke of Marlborough. He was therefore the half-brother of James Francis Edward Stuart, although there was an eighteen-year age gap between them. Berwick was a highly regarded professional soldier. Although he had been brought up in France from an early age, he served in James II's army in England and Ireland. After James II's death he chose (with his half-brother's permission) to adopt French nationality and served in the French army. In 1706, Louis XIV created him a marshal of France, the highest French military distinction. He was killed in action at the Siege of Philippsburg in 1734.

John Graham of Claverhouse, 1st Viscount Dundee (1647–1689)

CLAVERHOUSE was a professional soldier. In 1672, he joined an Anglo-Scots brigade and fought in Europe with first the French and then the Dutch army. On returning to Scotland in 1678, he commanded a company charged with the suppression of Presbyterian conventicles. He became much feared and hated in south-west Scotland, his main area of operation. Claverhouse remained loyal to James II in 1688, and in recognition James created him Viscount Dundee. When the Scottish Parliament accepted William of Orange as king in 1689, Claverhouse was declared a rebel and attempted to rally support from the Highland clans. His army, probably numbering less than 2,000 men, defeated government troops at Killiecrankie in July 1689, but Claverhouse himself was killed.

Alexander Gordon, Marquess of Huntly, later the 2nd Duke of Gordon (1678(?)–1728)

HUNTLY'S mother, daughter of the Duke of Norfolk, was a Catholic and a Jacobite, but his wife Lady Henrietta, daughter of Earl of Peterborough, was a Whig. Huntly brought 300 horsemen and 2,000 foot to join Mar at Perth, and was present at the Battle of Sheriffmuir, but went home soon afterwards. He surrendered in February 1716 and was imprisoned at Edinburgh but was pardoned when his father died in December 1716.

George Hamilton (aft.1658–aft.1728)

THE YOUNGER SON of an East Lothian heritor family, Hamilton joined the Dutch service at an early age and eventually rose to the rank of lieutenant-general. He was wounded fighting with the British forces at the Battle of Malplaquet (1709). Returning to Scotland, he was elected MP for the Fife constituency of Anstruther Easter Burghs in 1712. He was an inactive MP, an Episcopal Tory who was loyal to the Oxford ministry and followed Mar's lead in Scottish affairs. Mar believed that such a senior military officer would be an asset to the Jacobite rising, but Hamilton was not suited to the command of largely untrained troops. Mar blamed him, not entirely fairly, for the Jacobite failure at Sheriffmuir. His later life is obscure, but he is known to have died in exile.

John Hay of Cromlix, 1st Jacobite Duke of Inverness (1691–1740)

HAY was the third son of the 7th Earl of Kinnoull. He purchased a commission in the foot guards in 1714 and a year later married Marjorie Murray, daughter of the 5th Viscount Stormont and sister of the Earl of Mansfield. On 5 October 1718, he was created Earl of Inverness in the Jacobite peerage. In 1725, he was appointed the Jacobite Secretary of State, but resigned the post in 1727, upon which James elevated him to the titular Dukedom of Inverness.

William Mackintosh of Borlum (c.1657–1743)

A HIGHLANDER from near Loch Ness, Borlum was an educated man: a university graduate who was familiar with the work of Robert

Boyle, one of the founders of the Royal Society. He also had military experience in both the Dutch and French service, reaching the rank of colonel. In early October 1715, Borlum brought several hundred men to join the Earl of Mar at Perth. A few days later he set out with around 2,000 men on a bold expedition to cross the Firth of Forth towards Edinburgh. He subsequently marched his troops to the borders and eventually joined up with English Jacobites, but was forced to surrender at Preston in November 1715. Borlum was taken to London and imprisoned in Newgate but escaped the day before his trial and fled to France. He returned several times to Scotland before being finally captured there in 1727. He remained a state prisoner in Edinburgh Castle until he died in 1743. During his imprisonment Borlum wrote *An Essay on Ways and Means of Enclosing, Fallowing, and Planting Lands in Scotland, and That in Sixteen Years at Farthest*, published in 1729.

John Murray, 1st Duke of Atholl (1660–1724)

ATHOLL had vigorously opposed the Union of 1707, and until almost the last minute the Jacobites in France believed he would be willing to lead the 1715 rising. In the end he chose to support the government, although his brother Nairne and three of his sons were active Jacobites. Atholl had been the sheriff of Perthshire since 1695 and was appointed lord lieutenant in 1715. He had substantial landholdings throughout much of Perthshire as well as the regalities of Atholl and Dunkeld, which meant that he could hold courts with the power of life and death in that area. He was married twice and was the father of nineteen children, ten of whom survived to adulthood.

William Murray, 2nd Baron Nairne (c.1664–1726)

LORD WILLIAM MURRAY, younger son of the 1st Marquess of Atholl and brother of the 1st Duke of Atholl, became Lord Nairne when he married Margaret Nairne (1669–1747), the only daughter and heir of Baron Nairne. He was taken prisoner at the Battle of Preston and sentenced to death. Although he was pardoned, his title was forfeited. His son John, who but for the forfeiture would have been the 3rd Baron Nairne, was one of the Jacobite leaders in 1745. John's grandson William

Murray Nairne (1757–1830) was restored to the barony in 1824, becoming the 5th Baron Nairne. He married Carolina Oliphant, the daughter of a Perthshire Jacobite laird, well known as a writer of Scottish songs.

John St Clair, Master of Sinclair (1683–1750)

THE MASTER OF SINCLAIR was the eldest son of the 10th Lord Sinclair. A notoriously ill-tempered and quarrelsome man, he killed two fellow army officers while serving in Europe under the Duke of Marlborough. He was court-martialled for this in 1708 and sentenced to death but escaped and evaded capture until he was pardoned in 1712. Sinclair was quick to take up the Jacobite cause in 1715 and one of the first to join the camp in Perth, but he hated the Earl of Mar and had no faith in his ability to lead the rebellion. He was one of the few Jacobite officers with recent military experience and his raid on Burntisland was one of the few successful exploits of the 1715 campaign. He was present at the Battle of Sheriffmuir but apparently took no active part and left Perth shortly afterwards, going north with Huntly. In January 1716, he fled to Orkney and then to France. Sinclair remained in exile in France and the Low Countries until 1726, when a pardon meant that his life was no longer in danger. Although he later regained his property, he was never able to inherit his father's title, which remained attainted. His *Memoirs of the Insurrection in Scotland in 1715* is one of the most valuable accounts of the rebellion. Internal evidence indicates that it was written in haste in 1716, probably because Sinclair wanted to present his side of his quarrels with Mar while memories were still fresh. The manuscript was privately circulated among Jacobite sympathisers (including Sir Walter Scott) but was not published until 1858, because Sinclair's descendants were unwilling to expose his low opinion of his fellow Jacobites.

Henry St John, 1st Viscount Bolingbroke (1678–1751)

AS A MEMBER of the Tory government, Bolingbroke had been involved in secret negotiations with France before the Treaty of Utrecht was signed in March 1713. While in France he was in communication with the Jacobite court. When the Whigs came into office after the accession of George I his Jacobite contacts were revealed, and Bolingbroke realised he was in danger of being arrested for treason. Escaping to France in March 1715, he became James's secretary of state at the time the rising was being planned. On his return from Scotland James came to believe that Bolingbroke was responsible for the failure of the rising and dismissed him. Although he had been attainted for treason, he was eventually allowed to return to England in 1723.

Selected Further Reading

ALLARDYCE, J., *Historical Papers Relating to the Jacobite Period, 1699–1750* (Aberdeen: Printed for the New Spalding Club, 1895)

ANONYMOUS, *A Faithful Register of the Late Rebellion: Or, An Impartial Account of the Impeachments, Trials [&c.] of All Who Have Suffered for the Cause of the Pretender in Great Britain* (London, 1718)

ANONYMOUS, *A Collection of Original Letters and Authentick Papers, Relating to the Rebellion, 1715* (Edinburgh, 1730)

CANT, JAMES, *Memorabilia of the City of Perth: Containing, a Guide to Perth* (Perth: William Morison, 1806)

CULLEN, KAREN J., *Famine in Scotland: The 'Ill Years' of the 1690s* (Edinburgh: Edinburgh University Press, 2010)

DEVINE, T. M., *The Scottish Nation, 1700–2000* (London: Penguin, 2000)

DUNCAN, JEREMY, *Lost Perth* (Edinburgh: Birlinn, 2011)

EAGLES, JONATHAN and JAMES MAIDMENT, *The Chronicle of Perth* (Lampeter: Llanerch, 1996)

FARQUHAR, GEORGE T. S., *The Episcopal History of Perth, 1689–1894* (Perth: James H. Jackson, 1894)

FITTIS, ROBERT SCOTT, *Sketches of the Olden Times in Perthshire* (Perth: Printed at the Constitutional Office, 1878)

HUNT, COLIN A., *The Perth Hammermen Book (1518 to 1568)* (Perth: Incorporation of Hammermen, 1889)

LENMAN, BRUCE, *The Jacobite Risings in Britain 1689–1746* (London: Methuen, 1980)

MAIDMENT, JAMES, *The Spottiswoode Miscellany: A Collection of Original Papers and Tracts, Illustrative Chiefly of the Civil and Ecclesiastical History of Scotland* (Edinburgh: The Spottiswoode Society, 1844)

MARSHALL, THOMAS HAY, *The History of Perth* (Perth: John Fisher, 1849)

OLIPHANT, T. L. KINGTON, *The Jacobite Lairds of Gask* (London: Published for the Grampian Club by Charles Griffin and Co., 1870)

PATTEN, ROBERT, *The History of the Rebellion in the Year 1715. With Original Papers, and the Characters of the Principal Noblemen and Gentlemen Concern'd in It...*, 3rd edn (London: printed for J. Baker and T. Warner at the Black-Boy in Pater-Noster-Row, 1717)

PEACOCK, DAVID, *Perth: Its Annals and Its Archives*
(Perth: Thomas Richardson, 1849)

RAE, PETER, *The History of the Late Rebellion*, 2 volumes (Drumfries [sic], 1718)

REBEL, *A True Account of the Proceedings at Perth* (London: printed for J. Baker, 1716)

REID, S., *Sheriffmuir, 1715: The Jacobite War in Scotland*
(London. Frontline Books, 2014)

SCOTT, HEW, *Fasti Ecclesiae Scoticanae: The Succession of Ministers in the Church of Scotland from the Reformation* (Edinburgh: Oliver and Boyd, 1923), Volume IV: Synods of Argyll, and of Perth and Stirling

SINCLAIR, JOHN, *Memoirs of the Insurrection in Scotland in 1715, by John, Master of Sinclair, from the Original Manuscript in the Possession of the Earl of Rosslyn; with Notes by Sir Walter Scott* (Edinburgh: Abbotsford Club, 1858)

SINCLAIR-STEVENSON, C., *Inglorious Rebellion: The Jacobite Risings of 1708, 1715 and 1719* (London: Hamish Hamilton, 1971)

STAVERT, MARION L., *The Guildry Incorporation of Perth, 1200–2002*
(Perth: Guildry Incorporation of Perth, 2003)

STUART, A. FRANCIS, *News Letters of 1715–16, Printed from Original Papers in the Possession of C. E. S. Chambers, Edinburgh* (London: W. & R. Chambers, 1910)

SZECHI, DANIEL, *1715: The Great Jacobite Rebellion* (New Haven, CT: Yale University Press, 2006)

TAYLER, ALISTAIR and HENRIETTA TAYLER, *1715: The Story of the Rising* (London: Thomas Nelson and Sons, 1936)

TAYLER, H., *The Seven Sons of the Provost; A Family Chronicle of the Eighteenth Century Compiled from Original Letters, 1692 to 1761* (London: T. Nelson, 1949)

THOMSON, A., *Memoirs of the Jacobites of 1715 and 1745* (London: R. Bentley, 1845)

Note: *Electronic versions of the eighteenth- and nineteenth century books listed can be downloaded, free, from* **archive.org** *or* electricscotland.com.

INDEX

ABOUT THE AUTHOR

KATHLEEN LYLE was born and brought up in Perth, but now lives in Oxford. She studied biochemistry at St Andrews in the 1960s and then worked in publishing for many years, most recently as a freelance copy-editor of scientific and medical books. She is now retired. Her interest in history developed gradually over many years and eventually led to a master's degree in historical studies which she completed in 2018. When researching for her dissertation on the Jacobite occupation of Perth in 1715–16 she realised how much information about the 1715 rising there is to be found, not only in the local archives but also in rare eighteenth- and nineteenth-century publications. This book is the result.

THE PUBLISHER

Tippermuir Books Ltd (*est.* 2009) is an independent
publishing company based in Perth, Scotland.

OTHER TITLES FROM
TIPPERMUIR BOOKS

Spanish Thermopylae (Paul S. Philippou, 2009)

Battleground Perthshire
(Paul S. Philippou & Robert A. Hands, 2009)

Perth: Street by Street
(Paul S. Philippou and Roben Antoniewicz, 2012)

Born in Perthshire
(Paul S. Philippou and Robert A. Hands, 2012)

In Spain with Orwell (Christopher Hall, 2013)

Trust (Ajay Close, 2014)

Perth: As Others Saw Us (Donald Paton, 2014)

Love All (Dorothy L. Sayers, 2015)

A Chocolate Soldier (David W. Millar, 2016)

The Early Photographers of Perthshire
(Roben Antoniewicz and Paul S. Philippou, 2016)

Taking Detective Novels Seriously:
The Collected Crime Reviews of Dorothy L. Sayers
(Dorothy L. Sayers and Martin Edwards, 2017)

Walking with Ghosts (Alan J. Laing, 2017)

No Fair City: Dark Tales From Perth's Past
(Gary Knight, 2017)

The Tale o the Wee Mowdie that
wantit tae ken wha keeched on his heid
(Werner Holzwarth and Wolf Erlbruch,
translated by Matthew Mackie, 2017)

Hunters: Wee Stories from the Crescent:
A Reminiscence of Perth's Hunter Crescent
(Anthony Camilleri, 2017)

Flipstones (Jim Mackintosh, 2018)

Perth & Kinross: A Pocket Miscellany: A Companion for Visitors and Residents (Trish Colton, 2019)

God, Hitler, and Lord Peter Wimsey: Selected Essays, Speeches and Articles by Dorothy L. Sayers (Dorothy L. Sayers and Suzanne Bray (ed.), 2019)

The Piper of Tobruk: Pipe Major Robert Roy, MBE, DCM (Alice Soper, 2019)

The 'Gig Docter o Athole': Dr William Irvine & The Irvine Memorial Hospital (Rita Isles, 2019)

FORTHCOMING

A Collection of Bairnrhymes and Other Daftness (Stuart Patterson, 2019)

William Soutar: Collected Poetry (Kirsteen McCue and Paul S. Philippou (eds.), 2020)

'Where Sky and Summit Meet': Perthshire's Flying Heroes – Tales of Pilots, Airfields, Aeronautical Feats, and War (Ken Bruce, 2020)

BY LULLABY PRESS
(an imprint of Tippermuir Books)

A Little Book of Carol's (Carol Page, 2018)

All titles are available from bookshops and online booksellers.

They can also be purchased directly at
www.tippermuirbooks.co.uk

Tippermuir Books Ltd can be contacted at
mail@tippermuirbooks.co.uk

TIPPERMUIR
· BOOKS LIMITED ·